Growing Wings Self-Discovery Workbook:
17 Workshops to a Better Life
Volume One-Second Edition

from the Blue Wing Workshops Self-Discovery Series

Susan D. Kalior
M.A. in Education in Counseling
Human Relations and Behavior
B.S. in Sociology

Blue Wing Publications, Workshops, and Lectures
Tualatin, Oregon

Growing Wings Self-Discovery Workbook:
17 Workshops to a Better Life-Volume One
from the Blue Wing Workshops Self-Discovery Series
Copyright©2008 by Susan D Kalior
Blue Wing Workshops Copyright©2001 by Susan D Kalior
First Printing: February 2008
Second Printing: March 2015
ISBN 978-0-9795663-2-5

Published by Blue Wing Publications, Workshops, and Lectures
Cover Design by Laura C. Keyser
Logo by Sara C. Roethle
Author Photo by Stephen R. Roethle

Blue Wing Publications, Workshops, and Lectures
sdk@bluewingworkshops.com
www. bluewingworkshops.com
Readers' comments are welcomed.

Other Books by Susan D. Kalior

Growing Wings Self Discovery Workbook-Vol 2: 18 Workshops to a Better life: Exploring the Multi-faceted Self

The Other Side of God: The Eleven Gem Odyssey of Being

The Other Side of Life: The Eleven Gem Odyssey of Death

Warriors in the Mist: A Medieval Dark Fantasy

The Dark Side of Light: A Medieval Time Travel Fantasy

Johnny, the Mark of Chaos (Tazmark Dark Fantasy Series)

Jensea, an Angel's Touch (Tazmark Dark Fantasy Series)

Manufactured in the United States of America

Dedication

This workbook is dedicated to
all those who opened their lives to me.

Acknowledgements

Thanks to those whose invaluable feedback made this workbook all it could be: Mark Kalior, Matt Keyser, Karlyn Myers, Linda Post, and Dr. Cyndi Myers. I also want to thank the deeply talented Dr. Cyndi Meyers for healing my chronic back pain and extreme tendonitis, enabling me to put in the many writing hours needed to complete this project. Thanks to Robert V. Kalior for his infinite wisdom. Thanks to Laura C. Keyser for the cover design, Sara C. Roethle for her proofreading skills, and Stephen R. Roethle for the author photograph. Thanks to Jennifer Kalior, and Helen Levison for believing in me. And, as always, special thanks to my greatest cheerleader, my sister, Cindy Kalior.

Table of Contents

Introduction to Self-Discovery

From the moment we are born, there is a general indoctrination¹ into the precepts of those who raise us, and the world in which we live. It is understandable that the personal truth of who we each are as unique individuals would get challenged, covered, mangled, marred, and worst of all—forgotten.

Being true to one's self is key to coming into fruition. This means walking your own path, your own way. However, sometimes it is hard to be true to yourself if outside influence has obscured your sense of who you are. Sometimes, who we think we are is a reflection of other people's subjective opinions and collective agreement, and not the deep down us, often un-recognized and seldom celebrated.

In the story, *Little Red Riding Hood*, we are warned not to stray from the path already paved by the social group, or the big bad wolf will get us. While it is necessary to conjoin in a certain set of agreements and social rules that allow a community to function successfully, expression of individuality is paramount. If we cannot be who we are, we begin to display signs of distress: be it withdrawal, depression, bursts of anger, drinking one's self to sleep, or a myriad of other negative behaviors. This unhappiness affects those around us. Eventually, the distress ripples out to the community and the world.

We are further 'submerged' by the commercial world's use of the mass media to decree how we should look and act, and what services or products we should buy to attain happi-ness. After awhile, it is difficult to know if we are striving to become the image that we are expected to be, or if we are striving to become who we really are, which is generally not en-couraged. Once this is discerned, the next step is to become ourselves in the face of a social atmosphere that may not agree, and further exude false authority to judge our worth.

In this self-discovery workbook, you will have an opportunity to discover your unadorned essence so exquisite in worth, it defies all judgment, even your own. Your quintessential self, like the snowflake, is unique to all. If the way you move through life reflects that uniqueness, you will be in your own flow, following the beat to your own drum, and thus experience a brighter, freer life. And just as your repressed self can affect all around you, so too can the expressive freed self.

Each workshop will allow you to explore who you truly are, once all the imposed masks of others are removed from your face. And when you see that true face, it is this author's hope and belief that you will weep with joy, and embrace a new and better way of living.

1. Brainwashing

1

WORKSHOP GUIDELINES

*This workbook will help you explore who you are at *this time* in your life. It is important to fill in the date. A year from now, or a year ago, answers might be different. Reviewing the workbook from time to time often resurrects insights and inspiration, and can prove a wonderful asset to keep as a revered journal.

*Write directly in the book. Use a pencil that you may change answers as needed. Exploring self is like journeying through layers. You might be writing an answer, when a deeper truth arises, and crossing previous answers out in pen can prove messy and hard to read later. Feel free to use colored pencils, especially in exercises that require drawings. Drawings are not about good art. They are tools to help you see yourself.

*Do not skip the **Relaxation and Creative Visualization Experience** at the end of each workshop. This is perhaps the most important part of the workshop. Initial exploration through question and answer opens the door. The Creative Visualization experience is about walking through that door to discover personal truths that lie beyond conscious analysis. In the depths of our incorporeal being, the purest insights can be found, as well as a kind of universal wisdom. General guidelines are provided; however, feel free to diverge into your own experience whenever the flow takes you there. Trust that you will experience what you need in order to be a healthier, wiser, and more balanced person.

The **Relaxation and Creative Visualization Experience** requires instrumental music. Music selection is important. Select instrumental music that makes you feel good: classical, new age, or any music that is gentle, sweeping, or of dynamic beauty. This kind of music tends to initiate emotional catharsis, catalyze insight, and spark experiences that promote positive life change. If you have selected music that you have not yet heard, listen to it before using it with the Relaxation and Creative Visualization Exercise. It is essential that you find the music emotionally moving and not irritating. You can use the same music for each Relaxation and Creative Visualization Experience, or you can change it as you please.

*It is suggested that you complete no more than one workshop per day that the full benefit is reaped. However, if something inside you calls to complete more than one workshop per day, trust yourself. Make the most of each workshop, taking time to have a powerful experience with each one.

*It is suggested that you do not skip workshops, or do them out of order. They are designed as a progression, leading to your core self. However, if you sense that you are not ready to do a particular workshop, by all means, skip it.

*Before answering questions, search your mind and heart honestly. Set the intent to understand yourself better. The deeper you probe and the more honest your answers, the more you will discover about yourself. No one ever need see this Workbook. It is yours and yours alone.

*It is suggested that you have a supplementary journal for more extensive writing. A spiral notebook works nicely. Simply note in the workbook, See Journal, page 1 etc. This will allow you to extend any exercise that might help you further explore yourself, or answer at length if you choose.

*Do not skip the **Healing and Balancing Exercises.** They are invaluable. Suggestions are made for hand placement, however, feel free to place your hands where they feel best: crown of head, forehead, base of throat, heart, base of breastbone, or just below the navel.

***These workshops are not designed to replace other forms of therapy. If you feel you need therapy, it is suggested that you seek a therapist. If you are in therapy, it is suggested that you consult with your therapist regarding this workbook.**

*These workshops are the culmination of the author's years in the following: higher education, extracurricular training, extensive experience as a psychotherapist, sociological studies, and decades of facilitating self-discovery workshops. However, the self-discovery process works best when you trust your own sense of things. Therefore, always respond in a manner healthy to yourself.

Glossary of Common Terms for this Workbook

Self-actualization: The process of growing into one's full potential.

Significant Others: Key people in one's life, such as parent, sibling, mate, relative, or friend.

Social programming: Ideas we get from others, but assume as our own.

Mass Media: Newspapers, magazines, internet, radio, television, and the big screen.

Cerebral Nature: People with cerebral natures experience life primarily through thinking.

Emotional Nature: People with emotional natures experience life primarily through feeling.

Physical Nature: People with physical natures experience life primarily through action.

Effective Listening: Summarizing another person's behavior or words.

Constructive Self-Expression: Describing the situation that incites an emotion, stating what the emotion is, and why that emotion is felt.

Intrinsic Self-Worth: Self-worth apart from outside forces. One's worth is inherent.

Synchronicity: Every event has meaning, no matter how random it might appear. Each event fits into the larger scheme of things that create the tapestry of life.

Materials Needed

Pencils, colored pencils, spiral notebook, a machine that plays music.

THE BOOK OF

Adanya Adeline Rose
(YOUR NAME)

Date _March 9ᵗʰ, 2021_

WORKSHOP ONE
KNOW YOUR NATURE

We all have a basic nature comprised of various psychological traits. Being oblivious to our nature leads to a sort of bumbling through life, helpless to create positive personal change. Understanding and accepting our nature is essential to respectful self-acceptance. Likewise, understanding and accepting the nature of others, fosters better relationships with mates, family, and friends.

Fill in the answers below. There are no bad answers. Your answers merely reflect who you are _right now_ in your life. You are a unique individual, and no one else in the world is exactly like you. No one else has had the exact same experiences as you. No one can know you or understand you better than you can know or understand yourself. Everything you think and feel is valid.

List ten non-physical qualities that best describe you at this time in your life. Examples: shy, assertive, generous, dominating, submissive, insensitive, thoughtful, fearful, anxious, exuberant, quick-tempered, patient, wise, spiritual, adventurous, charitable, angry, judgmental, sensitive, playful, giving and loving, or anything else that comes to mind.

1. Hurt P
2. Angry P
3. Emotional N
4. Tired P
5. Bored P

6. Confused N
7. Scared N
8. Hypercritical N
9. Fake P
10. Weak N

Next to the traits you have listed, place a P for what you feel is a positive trait for you at this time in your life and an N for what you feel is a negative trait for you at this time in your life.

Note* A seemingly negative trait can be positive _for you_ at _this time_ in your life. Example: you have allowed people to take advantage of you. Now your anger has risen and you are more guarded. You are actually feeling better because you no longer "give yourself away." In this case, being angry is a positive trait. Conversely, a seemingly positive trait can be negative _for you_. Example: You are giving and loving _all the time_, and you are emotionally drained. In this case, being charitable _all the time_ is a negative trait.

If you placed a P for positive, next to what would normally be deemed a negative trait, explain.

1. *_____Hurt_____ is often considered a negative trait, but it is
   (list trait)

positial for me at this time in my life because __it is the reason for my__
__self journey I am on.__ .

2. *_____Angry_____ is often considered a negative trait, but it is
   (list trait)

positial for me at this time in my life because __it has been protecting me__
__from those who wish harm__ .

If you placed an N for negative, next to what would normally be deemed a positive trait, explain.

1. *_____Emotional_____ is not good for me now because __it has__
   (list trait)

__drained me.__ .

2. *_____ is not good for me now because _____
   (list trait)

_____ .

We all have diverse natures, from vastly different to fairly similar. Some people are more assertive than others, and some more passive. Some like to plan, others prefer spontaneity. Sometimes aspects of our nature seem to work against us. Below are several examples.

Example: If you have a dominating nature, you might accomplish tasks well, but be resented by others because they don't feel that their ideas are respected. Modifying that trait might entail abdicating to someone else's ideas on occasion. Your nature as a competent leader remains, yet it is tweaked so that others too can have their day in the sun.

Example: If you have a passive nature and like to please others, you might be liked, yet feel oppressed because your own needs go unmet. Modifying that trait might involve saying to yourself frequently, "I matter too." This, over time, could give you the courage to speak up for yourself, instead of living behind a safe, but uncomfortable mask. Your sweet and unassuming nature remains, yet it is tweaked so that you too can have your day in the sun.

Example: A "leap before you look" nature might result in exciting experiences, but also land you in undesirable circumstances. Modifying this trait might entail waiting one day before acting impulsively on *important* decisions. Your free-spirited, spontaneous nature remains, yet it is tweaked to add stability to your life.

Only you can determine if aspects of your nature seem to work against you, and if modification might improve your life.

1. *List a trait that you might like to modify. Disorganized.

In what way would you like to modify it? Immediately picking up after myself. Keeping areas clean as not doing so overwhelms me.

How might modifying this trait help *you*?
I'll find stuff and my ADHD won't spike.

2. *List another trait that you might like to modify. Dissapointed.

In what way would you like to modify it? Being able to say "This situation sucks" and not dwell on it.

How might modifying this trait help *you*?

3. *List another trait that you might like to modify. Hypercritical

In what way would you like to modify it? Changing my mindset about "mistakes" Therapy, writing and correcting negative thoughts

How might modifying this trait help *you*?
Less stress/breakdowns, build self-esteem part of my self journey

It is equally important to recognize and be proud of traits you possess.

1. *List a trait that you are proud to possess. _____

How does this trait help you? _____

2. *List another trait that you are proud to possess. _____

How does this trait help you? _____

3. *List another trait that you are proud to possess. _____

How does this trait help you? _____

_____.

Who you are is not set in stone, for even as who you are is uncovered and beheld—you are a living, growing, changing being. So, for now, let this be one of your personal sayings.

I am _____ and _____
                (positive trait)   (positive trait)

and _____ and I love myself.
                (positive trait)

Cerebral, Emotional, and Physical Natures

Every human has thoughts, feelings, and a body. However, some of us are more cerebral, emotional, or physical than others. Whatever our inclination, it will be the way we are pre-disposed to experience and deal with life. While of course, we utilize all three, one is often the channel for the other two. Example: Emotions for a person with a cerebral nature are ex-pressed primarily through conveying thoughts. Emotions for a person with an emotional na-ture are expressed primarily by conveying feelings. Emotions for a person with a physical na-ture are expressed primarily through action.

Once we identify our primary and secondary nature, as emotional, cerebral, or physical, we will begin to understand "the kind" we are, and perhaps, even "the kind" our significant oth-ers are. Sometimes, there is a close runner-up. One might be highly cerebral, but emotional expression is generally valued more. Sometimes the difference is distinct. One might be so rational and logical that underlying feelings aren't even identified.

Our nature is what it is. Accepting our nature is important. We can adjust how we emotional-ly, physically, or mentally respond, but our primary way of responding, be it cerebral, emo-tional, or physical—will not change, nor should it.

The Cerebral Nature:

People with cerebral natures experience life primarily through thinking. Their rudder for life decisions is logical, rational, and reasonable. Though feelings might bubble beneath the sur-face, cerebrally natured people value mind over emotion, even if only a little. They are more comfortable trusting their thoughts than their feelings. Their first response to anything is an-alytical. Actions are taken after the analyzing process is complete. Emotions, though perhaps strong, will be subjected to logic and reason, and seldom be allowed to run rampant. Under-standing everything is important to them. They question, they wonder, they enjoy solving puzzles, and knowing what makes things work. Their favorite question is . . . why? On rare occasions, emotional expression or action might be taken before analysis can kick in. If two natures compete for first place, one or the other will come to the forefront at various times.

The Emotional Nature:

People with emotional natures experience life primarily through feeling. They are easily hurt and loved, easily depressed and uplifted. They can be inspirational, persuasive, enthusiastic, and capable of great compassion. They also can be hotheaded, drama queens and kings, or 'cry babies.' They make decisions based on how they feel. Even if they have a runner up cere-bral nature, the analytical process will take a backseat to underlying feelings. They might go shopping because it makes them feel good, even if traffic is bad. The joy of seeing a bird soaring in the sky might incite a walk around the neighborhood, even if chores await. They like inducing feeling in others as much as they feel it in themselves: be it joy, love, compassion, anger, sorrow, or guilt. Before making logical decisions, doing an unsavory task, or proceeding full steam ahead with anything, they often need time to feel. They need to express their trepidations, their hope, and their joy before anything else can happen. On rare occasions, logic or action might trump feelings. If two natures compete for first place, one or the other will come to the forefront at various times.

The Physical Nature
People with physical natures experience life primarily through action. They are movement oriented. They use action to express underlying feeling, and use their bodies to feel better. They choose physical release as a way to deal with emotions, and to think. Frustration and joy are handled by engaging in a hobby, task, exercise, sport, or physical expression such as punching a wall, or sexual union. If affection is stirred, doing something nice for their loved one is preferred to gushing emotion, or a dissertation on what that person means to them. They are more comfortable using their body as a gateway to emotional expression, and life choices. Often, they need to engage in a physical activity to work out feelings and thoughts. Or, they might engage in a physical activity to suppress what they do not want to think and feel. On rare occasions, emotional release or the analytical process might be pushed to the forefront. If two natures compete for first place, one or the other will come to the forefront at various times.

Rate the order in which you are inclined to experience life. 1, 2, and 3, even if you feel almost equally divided between two. Almost always, one nature is just a hair stronger.

Cerebrally_____   Emotionally_____   Physically_____

Accepting your nature will foster better feelings toward yourself.

If you are primarily emotional in nature, and you want to get up and sing in the middle of the night, but feel guilty because you have work in the morning . . . sing on—with joy.

If you are primarily cerebral in nature, and make a logical choice that fosters a safe feeling, even though another choice might offer more fun—respectfully accept your decision.

If you are primarily physical in nature, and find that competing in a sport is an emotional release that helps you better deal with thoughts and feelings late—know that it is just your way.

Awareness of our significant others' natures can improve relationships.

We are *used to* and *comfortable with* what we know. If those around us react differently, we have a tendency to be upset.

An emotional outburst might be most disconcerting to one with a cerebral nature. The cerebral person might deem the emotional person as overdramatic. Conversely, a logical response to a harsh occurrence can be most frustrating to one with an emotional nature. The emotionally natured person might deem the logical (cerebral) person—insensitive.

When we don't understand the natures of those around us, judgment is passed, tension increased, and generally, we take other people's actions—personally. However, opening one's mind to the nature of others can prove most rewarding.

If you are primarily emotional in nature, but your significant other is primarily cerebral in nature, you can expect that your significant other's initial response to anything will be a thinking one. If you want to go on a vacation, but your significant other wants to save money for retirement (while this might still be an issue for discussion) you can understand that your significant other's logical thinking is an act of his or her nature rather than a show of insensitivity to your needs.

If you are primarily cerebral in nature, but your significant other is primarily physical in nature, you can expect that your significant other's initial response to anything will be a physical one. If, when upset, your significant other wants to jog instead of talk about it—you will understand and not take it personally. Talking can come later.

If you are primarily physical in nature, and your significant other is emotional in nature, you can expect that your significant other's initial response to anything will be a feeling one. You will realize that your significant other generally needs time to wallow, complain, panic, or fume before taking action. You can be patient, knowing that after the emotional release, action will follow.

Though another's nature may prove challenging, every nature has a beautiful side. Think of a person whose nature frustrates you. Now, think of the beautiful side of their nature. State it below.

I am frustrated by this persons nature, however _____

_____

_____.

Your nature has a beautiful side too. What is the beauty of your particular nature?

_____

_____

_____.

Make an Altar.
This week begin making an altar to yourself. You can use a shelf, plant stand, or counter top. Find objects such as candles, colors, scents, fabrics, sentimental pictures, objects from your past—or objects with which you identify, such as a seashell, or a plastic action hero. These objects represent all the best of you, the beauties within that perhaps even others cannot see. This is your worship to yourself, very private. No one need know that the altar you are building is for yourself unless you choose to tell.

Whoever you are . . . whatever you are, is precious and need not be judged—but embraced.

Healing and Balancing Exercise for Accepting One's Nature. We all have healing ability—use it on yourself.

> **Place one hand over your heart.**
> **Place the other hand on the crown of your head.**
> **Concentrate deeply. Repeat silently or aloud for at least two minutes,**
> **"I am me, and that's okay."**

Your commitment of love and support towards yourself is now deepened.

Relaxation and Creative Visualization Exercise.

Lie in a comfortable position. Play *instrumental* music that makes you feel good: classical, new age, or music that is gentle, sweeping, or of dynamic beauty. When the music is playing, close your eyes. Inhale through your nose, and exhale through your mouth slowly, eight times. Visualize that you are inhaling the power of the universe, which purifies and attunes you physically, emotionally, mentally, and metaphysically. When you exhale, all the tensions and worries leave your body and go back into the universe where they dissolve and blend into the pure life force.

Tighten and loosen your muscles slowly in this order.

Feet. Tighten. Loosen. Take a slow, deep breath, and exhale.
Calves. Tighten. Loosen. Take a slow, deep breath, and exhale.
Thighs. Tighten. Loosen. Take a slow, deep breath, and exhale.
Hips and buttocks. Tighten. Loosen. Take a slow, deep breath, and exhale.
Back. Tighten. Loosen. Take a slow, deep breath, and exhale.
Arms. Tighten. Loosen. Take a slow, deep breath, and exhale.
Hands. Tighten. Loosen. Take a slow, deep breath, and exhale.
Neck and shoulders. Tighten. Loosen. Take a slow, deep breath, and exhale.
Face. Tighten. Loosen. Take a slow, deep breath, and exhale.

Then completely relax and take eight more slow, deep, breaths. Inhale the universal life energy through your nose and exhale tension through your mouth.

Set the intent: *Whoever I am, whatever I am, whatever I need, whatever is right for me—so be it. I open to insight. I open to receive.*

Now that you are completely relaxed, imagine that you are drifting down like a stone, sinking into deep waters of your being. It feels good, soothing, and freeing to escape outer world conflict, to be free of social judgment. You touch down gently in the deepest, truest part of yourself, a stunning underground cavern. As the music plays, you walk about in the deepest cavern of your being. Take time to explore your inner world. Observe, touch, listen, and feel. What colors do you see? What do the walls feel like? What do you hear? What is it like to be in this pure place?

Sense the healing energy that emanates all around you. Absorb the healing energy and replenish. Then, you come upon yourself as you truly are, in purity, beyond all acts, beyond judgment (even your own) far away from the mundane world. Behold this pure self. Do not judge what you see. You might see a light or shape. You might view physical definition. Have a positive experience with this pure self. Do not censor what comes to mind. This is your journey, so you cannot do it wrong.

As the music ends, absorb this purest part of you into who you are as a personality in the world. You now have this pure self in the forefront of your being to help calm you, reaffirm your worth, repel harmful energy, and exert personal power. Rest a few moments and bask in the experience.

Record your experience.

_____

_____

_____

_____

_____

_____

_____

_____

_____

_____

_____

_____

_____

_____

Draw a picture or symbol that summarizes your experience.

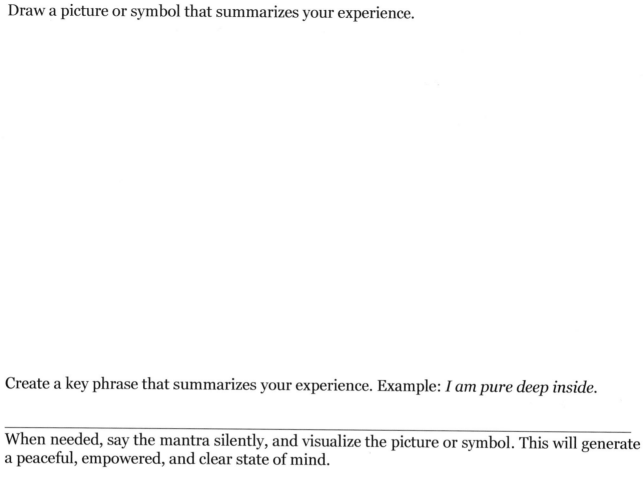

Create a key phrase that summarizes your experience. Example: *I am pure deep inside.*

_____

When needed, say the mantra silently, and visualize the picture or symbol. This will generate a peaceful, empowered, and clear state of mind.

Δ

Gem of Wisdom

*In the bounty of your own ageless, timeless quintessence
there is comfort, beauty, and unconditional love,
independent of the outside world.
The folly of humans is that they tend to reach 'out'
away from themselves to find the kind of comfort
that can best be found within—at the source.*

Live the Mystery

WORKSHOP TWO
DEALING WITH PRESSURES FROM THE OUTSIDE WORLD

While we all must tend to our health, care for our children, make a living or an arrangement where food and shelter are provided, and adhere to laws and community regulations—*the way* in which we do these things can make all the difference in the world. Without realizing it, we often go about our responsibilities in a rote-like manner programmed in us since birth. We are influenced by the social mores of our time, reinforced by the mass media. We are influenced by social groups and social institutions, by our schools and by our jobs. And perhaps, most of all, we are influenced by the immediate people in our lives: parents, family, mates, children, friends, and sometimes enemies.

Living in the world presents many challenges. Feeling pressured is often a way of life. Who we are as individuals against the backdrop of all we are expected to be, is easily dwarfed. Once we know, understand, and embrace who we uniquely are, we can be the leader of our life instead of a servant to the multitude. We can make choices that empower us, instead of choices that constrict us. We can fight for our individuality, instead of roping ourselves in to be like everyone else. In short, we can choose better ways to meet our needs, and we can weed out what we are trying to achieve that does not resonate with who we are. We *can* relieve the pressure.

This begins by understanding why we have placed importance on achieving certain things. We often feel we *must* achieve certain things or the world will end—*our* world will end, but will it? Or, is this something we assume because we have been programmed to assume it?

List some ways that you feel pressured by the outside world, things you *don't want to do*, but *feel you must*—and state why you feel pressured to achieve these things. While the following examples, for you, might be things you want to do, for others, they are a must. Example: *I feel pressured to look skinny so that people will think well of me. I feel pressured to earn a lot of money so that I can gain status. I feel pressured to always keep the house clean so that I will be deemed a good housekeeper.*

1. *I feel pressured to WORK IN A FIELD I DO NOT REALLY LIKE

   so that I CAN PROVIDE FOR MYSELF AND DASH.

2. *I feel pressured to VISIT MY PARENTS EVERY WEEKEND

   so that I AM NOT SEEN AS A BAD SON.

3. *I feel pressured to TAKE ON MORE THAN MY FAIR SHARE

so that _I CANNOT BE LET DOWN BY OTHERS_ .

4. *I feel pressured to_EARN MORE THAN MY PARTNER_

so that _SOCIETY DEEMS ME A GOOD PARTNER_ .

5. *I feel pressured to_HIDE HOW I FEEL_

so that _OTHERS WILL NOT LEAVE ME OR JUDGE ME_

6. *I feel pressured to_HIDE MY PAIN_

so that _I WILL NOT BE SEEN AS WEEK OR LYING_

7. *I feel pressured to_HANDLE DIRTY/FILTHY CHORES_

so that _DASH WONT NEED TO GET DIRTY_ .

8. *I feel pressured to_MANAGE EVERY THING_

so that _NOTHING GOES WRONG_ .

Review your answers. Note how many of your pressures involve self-worth. Apart from general survival and moderate comfort—the pressure to achieve certain things is often more about feeling worthy, than the achievement itself. Winning a prize is more about feeling special, than the value of the prize. However, not all pressures are motivated to gain self-worth. Sometimes our goals to achieve are motivated *from* self-worth.

When we do things to get a better sense of worth, rather than emanating *from* a sense of self-worth, the negative pressure mounts.

To take action in our lives motivated by *self-worth*, instead of taking action in our lives *to heighten or maintain self-worth*, we must further understand what currently feeds our sense of worth. Fill in the blanks below. Example: *I feel worthy when I make people happy because then I can feel good about myself. I feel worthy when I earn money because it makes me feel like I am being responsible.*

1. *I feel worthy when I _MAKE MY PARENTS HAPPY/PROUD_

because _I FEEL LIKE A GOOD SON_ .

2. *I feel worthy when I _HAVE A CLEAN HOME_

because _I FEEL MORE HAPPY AND LESS DEPRESSED_ .

3. *I feel worthy when I _GET DASH TO SMILE OR LAUGH_

because _SHE DID'NT FOR SO LONG AND IT MAKES ME HAPPY_

15

4. *I feel worthy when I _EARN A LOT OF MONEY_

because _I FEEL SUCCESSFULL_ .

5. *I feel worthy when I _AM FIT AND IN SHAPE_

because _IT PROVES TO ME THAT I CAN FIGHT MY DEPRESSION_ .

6. *I feel worthy when I _RECIEVE LOVE AND AFFECTION_

because _I NEVER RECIEVED IT WHEN I WAS YOUNGER_.

7. I feel worthy when I _BUY SOMETHING NICE_

because _IT GIVES ME A SENSE OF BEING FULFILLED_ .

8. *I feel worthy when I _TAKE CARE OF OTHERS_

because _I FEEL LIKE A PROTECTOR_ .

What did you just learn about yourself?

I HAVE SOME ISSUES WITH SELF WORTH
AND SELF ESTEEM.

_____ .

Once we understand what we require to feel worthy, it is time to discern which of our goals for achievement are due to pressures from the outside world, and which goals for achievement are truly in our own best interest.

There are achievements we seek that foster a sense of mental, physical, or psychological health. Example: We might have a goal to finish a work of art because it makes us feel great. Other achievements we seek foster resentment, anger, or sorrow. Example: We might take a prestigious job, even if we dislike that type of work.

The goals to achieve can be abstract: *It is my goal to be more assertive. It is my goal to pay more attention to my child. It is my goal to love myself more.* Or concrete: *It is my goal to lose ten pounds. It is my goal to buy a fancy car. It is my goal to travel to Europe.*

Or the goals to achieve can be simple: *It is my goal to get to work on time everyday. It is my goal to eat a salad with every dinner. It is my goal to read for one hour every night.* Or elaborate: *It is my goal to get a college degree. It is my goal to get this person to marry me. It is my goal to get the whole world to love me.*

All goals for achievement will generate a certain kind of tension. That is normal. Whether that tension is constructive or debilitating depends on the motivation behind the goal. The goal itself is not in question. Example: The goal to get a college degree, if motivated because one is eager to work in that field, yields a positive tension. The goal to get a college degree, if motivated by a need for approval, yields a negative tension.

While there is nothing wrong with achieving to feel worthy, operating from an already established good sense of self diminishes much pressure. If self-worth is not at stake, then the need to achieve comes from a place of self-love, enthusiasm, and joy. If self-worth is at stake, a sense of desperation prevails.

Of your goals: abstract and concrete, simple and elaborate—what you are trying to achieve that is motivated *to gain, or maintain self-worth?*

1. I am trying to _____.

2. I am trying to _____.

3. I am trying to _____.

4. I am trying to _____.

5. I am trying to _____.

6. I am trying to _____.

7. I am trying to _____.

8. I am trying to _____.

Of your goals: abstract and concrete, simple and elaborate—what you are trying to achieve *because you feel worthy?*

1. I am trying to _____.

2. I am trying to _____.

3. I am trying to _____.

4. I am trying to _____.

5. I am trying to _____.

6. I am trying to _____.

7. I am trying to _____.

8. I am trying to _____.

Now that you have separated what you are trying to do to gain, or maintain a sense of worth, from what you are trying to do because you *already* value yourself, state below some goals for achievement that you can release. Examples: *Because I am worthy no matter what, I can stop trying to impress everyone with my education. Because I am worthy no matter what, I can stop driving myself crazy keeping the house clean all the time. Because I am worthy no matter what, I can stop 'sleeping around' as a way to affirm my desirability.*

1. *Because I am worthy no matter what, I can stop _____

_____.

2. *Because I am worthy no matter what, I can stop _____

_____.

3. *Because I am worthy no matter what, I can stop _____

_____.

4. *Because I am worthy no matter what, I can stop _____

_____.

5. *Because I am worthy no matter what, I can stop _____

_____.

Now think of some *new* goals for achievement that you can move toward because you know that you *are* worthy. Example: *Because I am worthy, I am going to work toward having a job that I like. Because I am worthy, I am going to exercise because it makes me feel better. Because I am worthy, I am going to take some time to have fun.*

1. *Because I am worthy, I am going to _____

_____.

2. *Because I am worthy, I am going to _____

_____.

3. *Because I am worthy, I am going to _____

_____.

Healing and Balancing Exercise to Locate Self Worth. We all have healing ability—use it on yourself.

> **Place one hand over your heart.**
> **Place the other hand on the crown of your head.**

Concentrate deeply. Repeat silently or aloud for at least two minutes, "My worth is always with me—it cannot be taken."

You can now relax, knowing that your self-worth is never at stake, nor has it ever been.

Relaxation and Creative Visualization Exercise.

Lie in a comfortable position. Play instrumental music that makes you feel good: classical, new age, or music that is gentle, sweeping, or of dynamic beauty. When the music is playing, close your eyes. Inhale through your nose, and exhale through your mouth slowly, eight times. Visualize that you are inhaling the power of the universe, which purifies and attunes you physically, emotionally, mentally, and metaphysically. When you exhale, all tensions and worries leave your body and go back into the universe where they dissolve and blend into the pure life force.

Tighten and loosen your muscles slowly in this order.

Feet. Tighten. Loosen. Take a slow, deep breath, and exhale.
Calves. Tighten. Loosen. Take a slow, deep breath, and exhale.
Thighs. Tighten. Loosen. Take a slow, deep breath, and exhale.
Hips and buttocks. Tighten. Loosen. Take a slow, deep breath, and exhale.
Stomach. Tighten. Loosen. Take a slow, deep breath, and exhale.
Back. Tighten. Loosen. Take a slow, deep breath, and exhale.
Arms. Tighten. Loosen. Take a slow, deep breath, and exhale.
Hands. Tighten. Loosen. Take a slow, deep breath, and exhale.
Neck and shoulders. Tighten. Loosen. Take a slow, deep breath, and exhale.
Face. Tighten. Loosen. Take a slow, deep breath, and exhale.

Then completely relax and take eight more slow, deep breaths. Inhale the universal life energy through your nose and exhale tension through your mouth.

Set the intent: *Whoever I am, whatever I am, whatever I need, whatever is right for me—so be it. I open to insight. I open to receive.*

Now that you are completely relaxed, give yourself over to the music that is playing. Focus inward to your vast self, as vast as the universe. Journey within. You come upon the part of you that feels negatively pressured. It is layered in clothing so thick that you cannot see the real you beneath. These layers are what you expect of yourself and what others expect of you that are not in your own best interest. Feel the pressure. Then, because you are too worthy to put yourself through this, you remove these layers one by one, labeling the expectation that each layer represents. Example: The first layer might be the expectation to be a perfect parent. When you remove that layer, you remove that expectation. The second layer might be that you feel you must never be sad. When you remove that layer, you remove that expectation, and so on, until all layers are removed. Then, in bareness, make peace with the self you see before you. Commit to championing the true you. You will no longer do things to gain approval. You will do things because they make you flourish inside yourself. Notice how it feels to be free of what metaphorically crushes you. Do not judge your experience, nor censor what comes to mind. This is your journey, so you cannot do it wrong.

As the music comes to an end, allow this newly unencumbered self to blend into you, to help calm you, reaffirm your worth, repel harmful energy, and exert personal power. Rest for a few moments and bask in the experience.

Record your experience.

_____

_____

_____

_____

_____

_____

_____

_____

_____

_____

_____

_____

_____

_____

_____

Draw a picture or symbol that summarizes your experience.

Create a key phrase that summarizes this experience. Example: "I am free to be me."

_____

When needed, say the mantra silently, and visualize the picture or symbol. This will generate a peaceful, empowered, and clear state of mind.

Δ

Gem of Wisdom
There are many aspects to our being—
among them is a wise inner sage.
Trust that wise self to bring
you into fruition and guide you 'home.'

Live the Mystery

Date_____

WORKSHOP THREE
FEELING TRAPPED

We often feel trapped in our lives. Trapped by our situations, by our environment, by the people around us, by feelings of inadequacy, or by responsibilities. Whether we realize it or not, our sense of entrapment is held in place by our perceptions of ourselves, others, and the world around us. In short, our traps are self-made even though outside people and events might contribute to that trap. In this workshop, we will examine what holds our trap in place, what oppresses us and why, and most importantly, how to dissolve the trap and gain a sense of freedom.

The choices we make either confine us or free us. Accepting that we can alter our life if we choose is essential to creating positive life change. From the ashes rises the great phoenix bird. When you are ready to rise and spread your wings, nothing and no one can stop you.

In what ways do you feel trapped? Examples: *I feel trapped by my job. I feel trapped by my spouse. I feel trapped by my financial situation. I feel trapped by my monotonous life. I feel trapped by my friend. I feel trapped by my lack of skills. I feel trapped by my negative thinking. I feel trapped by my anxiety. I feel trapped by my shyness.*

1. I feel trapped by_____.

2. I feel trapped by_____.

3. I feel trapped by_____.

4. I feel trapped by_____.

5. I feel trapped by_____.

6. I feel trapped by_____.

7. I feel trapped by_____.

8. I feel trapped by_____.

Components, like bars to a jail cell, keep our traps in place. In order to dissolve the trap, we must examine these components. These components at first glance, might seem like they involve things outside yourself. Example: *"The components to my trap are my spouse, my neighborhood, my job, my pushy relatives, and my noisy house.* However, upon closer examination, those components outside yourself will reflect the components within yourself that keep your trap in place. Example: The component 'my spouse,' as a reason for feeling trapped is merely a beard for marital problems, and marital problems have roots such as the lack of communication. Hence, because one does not communicate, the troubled marriage remains the same. Therefore, a component to the trap would be *unwillingness to communicate*. There are often, but not always, several components to each thing that makes us feel trapped.

Restate below what makes you feel trapped, and then state what the root components might be. Example: *I feel trapped by my job—the root components are fear of change and fear of failure. I feel trapped by my shyness—the root components are fear of rejection, and lack of self-esteem.* Examples of Root Components: won't communicate, low self-esteem, a bitter attitude, intolerance, too tolerant, fear of conflict, too confrontational, fear of change, lack of stability, need for approval, too cocky, too shy, insecurity, fear of success, fear of failure, fear of rejection, need to please, need to criticize, can't make a stand, bottle my emotions, emotions run rampant, or anything else that comes to mind.

1. *I feel trapped by _____.

The root components are: _____.

2. *I feel trapped by _____.

The root components are: _____.

3. *I feel trapped by _____.

The root components are: _____.

4. *I feel trapped by _____.

The root components are: _____.

5. *I feel trapped by _____.

The root components are: _____.

6. *I feel trapped by _____.

The root components are: _____.

7. *I feel trapped by _____.

The root components are: _____.

8. *I feel trapped by _____.

The root components are: _____.

Many of these components are fear based. Our fears keep us trapped. Unwillingness to communicate is often motivated by a fear of confrontation. A bitter attitude is often motivated by fear of being hurt. The need to please is often motivated by the fear of rejection.

This next exercise will help you identify what you fear and how it keeps you trapped. Fill in the answers below. Examples: *Because I fear expressing myself, the consequence is that nobody understands me. Because I won't do things the way I want to, the consequence is that I feel oppressed. Because I fear that I am inadequate, the consequence is that I won't try new things.*

1. *Because I fear _____, the consequence is

_____.

2. *Because I fear _____, the consequence is

_____.

3. *Because I fear _____, the consequence is

_____.

4. *Because I fear _____, the consequence is

_____.

5. *Because I fear _____, the consequence is

_____.

6. *Because I fear _____, the consequence is

_____.

7. *Because I fear _____, the consequence is

_____.

8. *Because I fear _____, the consequence is

_____.

State below what personal changes *you can make* to dissolve your trap. Example: *If I step past my fear of rejection, then my life would improve because I could make some friends. If I get past my fear of confrontation, my life would improve because unsettled issues could finally get resolved. If I could step past my fear of change, I could go back to school to get a new career.*

1. *If I step past my fear of _____,

then my life would improve because _____

_____.

2. *If I step past my fear of _____,

then my life would improve because _____

_____.

3. *If I step past my fear of _____,

then my life would improve because _____

_____.

4. *If I step past my fear of _____,

then my life would improve because _____

_____.

5. *If I step past my fear of _____,

then my life would improve because _____

_____.

6. *If I step past my fear of _____,

then my life would improve because _____

_____.

7. *If I step past my fear of _____,

then my life would improve because _____

_____.

Replace self-defeating internal dialogue with empowering dialogue. Examples: *I have feared communicating, but now I am ready to express myself.* Or, *I have feared change, but now I am ready for a wonderful new adventure!* Even if you are not quite ready, try it on for size.

1. *I have feared _____

but now I am ready _____.

2. *I have feared _____

but now I am ready _____.

3. *I have feared _____

but now I am ready _____.

4. *I have feared _____

but now I am ready _____.

5. *I have feared _____

but now I am ready _____.

6. *I have feared _____

but now I am ready _____.

7. *I have feared _____

but now I am ready _____.

In summary: you must change, if your life is to change. Though these changes may be gradual, and take time to develop—taking steps, even small ones, can generate the most wonderful feeling of freedom.

Once the changes are made within you, it is only a matter of time before they manifest around you.

Healing and Balancing Exercise for Freeing Self from Traps. We all have healing ability—use it on yourself.

> **Place one hand at the base of breastbone.**
> **Place the other hand on the crown of your head.**
> **Concentrate deeply. Repeat silently or aloud for at least two minutes,**
> **"I am stronger than I know; it's easy to be free."**

Strength and assurance now fill you up from the inside, out.

Relaxation and Creative Visualization Exercise

Lie in a comfortable position. Play instrumental music that makes you feel good: classical, new age, or music that is gentle, sweeping, or of dynamic beauty. When the music is playing, close your eyes. Inhale through your nose, and exhale through your mouth slowly, eight times. Visualize that you are inhaling the power of the universe, which purifies and attunes you physically, emotionally, mentally, and metaphysically. When you exhale, all the tensions and worries leave your body and go back into the universe where they dissolve and blend into the pure life force.

Tighten and loosen your muscles slowly in this order.

Feet. Tighten. Loosen. Take a slow, deep breath, and exhale.
Calves. Tighten. Loosen. Take a slow, deep breath, and exhale.
Thighs. Tighten. Loosen. Take a slow, deep breath, and exhale.
Hips and buttocks. Tighten. Loosen. Take a slow, deep breath, and exhale.
Stomach. Tighten. Loosen. Take a slow, deep breath, and exhale.
Back. Tighten. Loosen. Take a slow, deep breath, and exhale.
Arms. Tighten. Loosen. Take a slow, deep breath, and exhale.
Hands. Tighten. Loosen. Take a slow, deep breath, and exhale.
Neck and shoulders. Tighten. Loosen. Take a slow, deep breath, and exhale.
Face. Tighten. Loosen. Take a slow, deep breath, and exhale.

Then, completely relax and take eight more slow, deep breaths. Inhale the universal life energy through your nose and exhale tension through your mouth.

Set the intent: *Whoever I am, whatever I am, whatever I need, whatever is right for me—so be it. I open to insight. I open to receive.*

Now that you are completely relaxed, give yourself over to the music. Focus inward to your vast self, as vast as the universe. Journey within. You come upon yourself in a jail cell. The bars are composed of things you fear. Take note of how this trapped part of you appears behind the bars, the panic, the sadness, the dejection. Focus on your intrinsic value as a human being. Summon the courage and conviction to free yourself to grow into your full potential. Touch a jail bar. Identify the fear that the jail bar represents. Then grasp the bar, feeling love and respect for yourself. The bar dissolves. Repeat this with each bar until all the bars are gone, and your trapped self is free. As the music plays, your freed self blends into you and gives you wings. You find yourself flying in the sky like a bird. Experience freedom. This is your journey, so you cannot do it wrong.

As the music ends, you feel metaphorical wings on your back. Rest a few moments and bask in the experience.

Record your experience.

_____

_____

_____

_____

_____

_____

_____

_____

_____

_____

_____

_____

_____

Draw a picture or symbol that summarizes your experience.

Create a key phrase that summarizes this experience. Examples: "I have the power to break my traps."

_____

When needed, say the mantra silently, and visualize the picture or symbol. This will generate a peaceful, empowered, and clear state of mind.

Δ
Gem of Wisdom
The outside world is a reflection of the inside world.
Change what goes on within you,
and you will change what goes on around you.

Live the Mystery

4

WORKSHOP FOUR
DEALING WITH GUILT

The premise of guilt is that we somehow have failed, either others or ourselves. Sometimes heavy guilt is triggered over seemingly small events such as stepping on a flower, to unbearable events such as losing a child. Most guilt revolves around feeling bad that because of our action, or inaction, a living creature (sometimes ourselves) was hurt in some manner, emotionally, physically or both. Guilt, when fueled, can plunge us into deep despair. Unresolved guilt can lead to unhealthy forms of self-punishment, from stubbing a toe to substance abuse. Self-worth *must* be rescued if guilt is to be absolved. To this end, we must examine the roots of our guilt. **If you are currently in therapy, it is advised that you consult your therapist before proceeding with this workshop.**

Review your life. Remember the times you felt guilty. Fill in the blanks. I feel guilty about . . .
Examples: *I feel guilty about being mean to my uncle before he died. I feel guilty about stealing from the store. I feel guilty about not having the courage to stand up for my friend.*

1. I feel guilty about _____

_____.

2. I feel guilty about _____

_____.

3. I feel guilty about _____

_____.

4. I feel guilty about _____

_____.

5. I feel guilty about _____

_____.

6. I feel guilty about _____

_____.

7. I feel guilty about _____

_____.

The exercise below will help deflect guilt. If you need it, do it now. Otherwise, it will appear again before the Relaxation and Creative Visualization Experience.

Healing and Balancing Exercise to Deflect Guilt. We all have healing ability—use it on yourself.

> **Place one hand at the base of your breastbone.**
> **Place the other hand over your heart.**
> **Concentrate deeply. Repeat silently or aloud for at least two minutes,**
> **"I am worthy, no matter what."**

You have rescued your self-worth; guilt slides away.

Now that we have identified what guilt we carry from the past, it is now time to identify the guilt we feel today when we do certain things. Fill in the blanks. I feel guilty when . . . Examples: *I feel guilty when I spend too much money. I feel guilty when I hurt someone's feelings. I feel guilty when I am late getting somewhere. I feel guilty when I am a coward.*

1. I feel guilty when_____

_____.

2. I feel guilty when_____

_____.

3. I feel guilty when_____

_____.

4. I feel guilty when_____

_____.

5. I feel guilty when_____

_____.

6. I feel guilty when_____

_____.

7. I feel guilty when_____

_____.

Of all these things you feel guilty about, did any involve mal-intent? Circle the best answer below.

none   some   a lot   almost all   all

We often build up cases against ourselves that don't hold much logic. Example: *My mom was dying in the hospital while I was out having a good time at the movies. Even though I didn't know she was dying, I should have been there. I should have. I am a bad person.* In cases like these, we mean no harm.

Other cases are more definitive regarding the part we might have played. Example: *I was mean to my sister at a time she needed support. She went downhill after that.* In this case, there is more to the story. Would one be mean for no reason? However, the biggest factor here is that the sister had many problems before the "mean" event occurred, and a complexity of events that built up to the point that she went downhill. Further, a complexity of events also led to other party "being mean." We can never be responsible for the choices others make. And it is even more important that we don't *judge* the choices others make. How can we know that a choice that seems bad is not what a person needs to catalyze future healing? How can we know what is truly meant for another human being, in life, or death? People make choices. We are not superior to any other, nor anyone to us. All we can do is feel our own way through the challenges of our lives, falling on knees, getting bruised once in a while, but coming out wiser and stronger. Always, always making our own choices.

When we do *intentionally* take action to hurt another, it is generally because we are retaliating somehow for something we feel was done to us. Guilt sets in when we regret our action. In this case, the lesson here is to stop judging others as the cause of our pain. Again, we make our own choices. If we have been hurt, we can change our lives for the better, instead of dwelling on those who hurt us. Even those who hurt us have their own life story, and will have to answer to their choices. No one can escape answering to the choices he or she made. No one. Our energy is better spent by growing wings and having a beautiful life.

If you need, repeat the **Healing and Balancing Exercise for Deflecting Guilt.** Otherwise, it will appear again before the Relaxation and Creative Visualization Experience.

> **Place one hand at the base of your breastbone.**
> **Place the other hand over your heart.**
> **Concentrate deeply. Repeat silently or aloud for at least two minutes.**
> **"I am worthy, no matter what."**

Self-worth is rescued; guilt slides away.

Describe the sensations in your body that guilt generates. Examples: nervous stomach, aching heart, headaches, sleepiness, anxiety, nausea.

_____

_____

In what ways do you deal with your guilt? Examples: drinking, distracting myself, blaming others, making myself sick, punishing myself, working harder, crying, apologizing, being grumpy, being depressed. You might have more than one answer.

I deal with my guilt by _____

_____.

What is the result of dealing with guilt in this or these ways?

_____

_____.

There is usually some key ideal that we have set for ourselves that if not met, triggers guilt. Examples: *I must be honorable. I must be successful. I must be good. I must get my parents approval. I must make everyone love me.*

If you could sum up the key ideal that triggers your guilt, what would it be?

_____.

If needed, repeat the **Healing and Balancing Exercise for Deflecting Guilt.** Otherwise, it will appear again before the Relaxation and Creative Visualization Experience.

Place one hand at the base of your breastbone.
Place the other hand over your heart.
Concentrate deeply. Repeat silently or aloud for at least two minutes,
"I am worthy no matter what."

Self-worth is rescued; guilt slides away.

We are human, frailties and all, in the dark much of the time. As we grow older, we have an opportunity to become *enlightened.* However, the most enlightened are often the same people who were once lost and confused in a shadowed past. It is never too late to shake off the dust and grow into our potential.

Sometimes our guilt stems from what we feel is a weakness in us. Example: We might feel that our child wouldn't have been hurt had we been more attentive. We might deem distraction a weakness.

What do you deem your greatest human frailty? Examples: fear of confrontation, too impulsive, too emotional.

_____

What problems does this frailty present? Example: *I fear confrontation so I have a lot of pent up resentment. I am so impulsive that I keep getting into trouble. I am so emotional that people withdraw from me.*

_____

_____.

There are positive sides to every frailty, and a gift in each. You might feel guilty for getting distracted, hence your child got hurt. Now, you might learn to be more focused in certain situations. And yet, that same distractive quality might save the life of drowning child at the lake because while your friend is talking to you, you are glancing about the scenery. Or, you might feel guilty that you did not put yourself in harm's way to save someone else's life. Now, you might review what you could have done that can be helpful in a future situation. And yet, that same sense of self-preservation also ensured that you'd be alive to raise your children. Or, you might feel guilty that you did not make a stand for someone you loved. But perhaps that needed to happen to catalyze you to work on your fear of speaking up. And yet, that inhibition might have inadvertently saved you from something else. Nothing is ever so black and white as it might seem to be. Beauty lies everywhere in everything. Synchronicity is ever present. Sometimes, we just need to read between the lines. And sometimes, we need to widen our scope of vision.

What is the positive side of your "so-called" frailty? Example: *My fear of confrontation is also my strength because it makes me a peacemaker. My impulsivity is also my strength because I have exciting adventures. Being very emotional is also my strength, because it reflects my empathic sensitivity, which gives me excellent intuition.*

My frailty is also my strength because _____

_____.

We are who we are, born into the world with specific physical, emotional, and mental characteristics, and into a particular environment and situation. These are the cards we are dealt. It takes much time to learn how to survive with the variables of who we are as individuals, the environment we are in, and the situations we encounter. There are ups and downs to every trait, environment, and situation. There are gifts in every tragedy. There are challenges in every walk of life. No one can be all things, to all people, all the time. It is virtually impossible. Therefore, it is to be expected that we will sometimes "fail," sometimes be weak in certain areas, and sometimes get very confused and frightened in this big and demanding world.

We are all doing our best. This does not mean that we don't have things to learn or some growing to do, but we can only *sense* our own way at any given moment. The act of thrashing self only generates negative repercussions.

Examining and coming to terms with the "failures" that our frailty seemingly caused—quells guilt.

What guilt evoking event do you deem your greatest failure? Examples: *My child got hurt because of me. I betrayed my spouse. I accidentally killed someone. I didn't stand up for my loved one. I wrongly accused someone.*

_____.

What was going on *inside* you and *around you* at the time? Example: Failure is: "I didn't stand up for my son." **At that time**, *it was important for me to be liked.* **For some reason I could not** *speak up in protest.* **I felt** *blocked.* **The sentence that always ran through my head then was,** *"Don't rock the boat."* **At that time, I felt pressured to** *get approval from others.* **My circumstance was** *that I was a young mother in a new town. I had no friends. I had no support system.* **The people around me** *seemed to be doing everything right. My sister seemed to be a perfect mother and everyone loved her. I was trying to measure up to her. I was trying to make things look right more than be right."* **The underlying feeling in all of this was** *inadequacy.*

Example: **My perceived failure was**: "I got in a car accident from driving drunk." **At that time,** *it was important for me to drink alcohol.* **For some reason, I could not** *stop drinking.* **I felt** *bad all the time, except for when I drank.* **The sentence that always ran through my head was,** *"I am no good."* **At that time, I felt pressured to** *make something of myself.* **My circumstance was** *that I was out of work and had been fired from my last job. I didn't have the money to go back to school. I had an eviction notice for the end of the month.* **The people around me** *kept criticizing, calling me irresponsible, saying I created my own situation.* **The underlying feeling in all of this was** *stupidity.*

My perceived failure was _____.

At that time, it was important for me _____

For some reason, I could not_____

_____.

I felt_____.

_____

The sentence that always ran through my head was, _____

_____.

At that time, I felt pressured to_____

_____.

My circumstance was _____

_____

_____

_____.

The people around me _____

_____.

The underlying feeling in all this was _____.

Every 'failing' presents an opportunity for ourselves and others to grow. Everyone "fails" and everyone can grow.

How have you "grown" or how can you grow as a result of this "failing?" Examples: _Because I felt guilty that I didn't stand up for my son, I forced myself thereafter to stand up for the ones I love. (Or, I can do this now). Because I felt guilty for my drunk driving accident, I got professional help and found healthy ways to deal with my stress. (Or, I can do this now)._

Because I feel guilty for my failing, I have grown, or can grow by _____

_____.

Gifts can be seen in everything, if examined closely. Next time you feel guilty, focus on the gifts. Often, events that we deem harsh can be the greatest contributor to our growth and the growth of those around us. While we never want to repeat that "failing," something important occurred whether we can see it or not. Life is balanced. There is no good without bad, no dark without light. Everything comes to equilibrium, eventually, always. It is natural law. No one is so powerful that he or she can alter another's course. It only _seems_ that way. We each have an elaborate metaphysical intent for living and dying. The people in our lives drive us to fulfill that intent. The people in our lives motivate us to become more than we are, even those we may not like so well. And as a person in the lives of others, we too motivate them to grow, even if they don't like us so well.

Sometimes we can forgive another more easily than we can forgive ourselves. Could you forgive another person for your identical "failing?" Why or why not?

_____

_____.

Allow yourself to accept your frailty and release the notion that you have failed. See that, for that time, you did the best you could—and that your action, then, was a way to survive. Forgive yourself as compassionately as you might another. Allow yourself to embrace your worth despite your "seeming" weakness, just as you might embrace the worth of another, despite theirs. We all struggle, and we have a right to grant ourselves and others time to learn by trial and error. We all need time to discover what actions work for us and what actions work against us. We need time to discover that _how we think_ affects every aspect of our lives.

The cornerstone of releasing guilt is realizing that worth is intrinsic. Each human has gifts and frailties that symbiotically interconnect to facilitate a great story. Any great work has dissonance as well as harmony. When we forgive our weaknesses, we more easily forgive others. No one is exempt from weakness. Deep down, we are all the same in our human make-up— weak and strong, frightened and brave, angry and loving.

Everyone in the world has faltered. We all do what we do, and have all done what we have done at any given moment based on hundreds of factors not always visible for analyzing. We are complex beings, and we are *always* doing what we feel we must to survive. We can look back and feel bad for something we have done, but if we went back to that exact moment with all the exact variables in place, (without hindsight) we would do the same again. If everything down to the minute detail was identical, we could not help it. There is a great gift we can give ourselves, and that is to accept that we are not bad. We are just doing our best to survive: physically, emotionally, mentally, and metaphysically. This does not mean our actions don't yield consequences that we might hate. This is part of the trial and error of learning what does and does not work for us. However, forgiving self is crucial to building a strong foundation of love and respect, not only for ourselves, but others.

Guilt generates opportunities for growth and insight—and can catalyze invaluable positive change in our lives. But holding onto guilt too long, or not using that guilt to make something beautiful happen in the future, only digs into our conscience until we are too hurt to live constructively.

The gift my guilt gave me, or the gift my guilt can give me is_____

_____

_____.

Who we are is made up of weaknesses and strengths, all rooted in innocence. And everything that has flowered from those roots carries its own kind of beauty—hence weaknesses, and the darker more shadowed areas of self also play important parts in the makeup of who we are, who we attract into our lives, and the adventures yet before us.

Who among us knows, that stripped of ideas ingrained in us from this or that, that whatever has happened was perhaps exactly what needed to happen to bring growth to a story and unexpected beauty to a life. Bow reverently before your life story, for it has meaning. Allow yourself to come into fruition. Just as a seed eventually generates a beautiful flower, so will you.

Healing and Balancing Exercise for Deflecting Guilt
If you have not yet done it, now is the time. We all have healing ability—use it on yourself.

Place one hand at the base of your breastbone.
Place the other hand over your heart.
Concentrate deeply. Repeat silently or aloud for at least two minutes,
"I am worthy no matter what."

Self-worth is rescued; guilt slips away.

Relaxation and Creative Visualization Exercise.
Lie in a comfortable position. Play instrumental music that makes you feel good: classical, new age, or music that is gentle, sweeping, or of dynamic beauty. When the music is playing, close your eyes. Inhale through your nose, and exhale through your mouth slowly, eight times. Visualize that you are inhaling the power of the universe, which purifies and attunes

you physically, emotionally, mentally, and metaphysically. When you exhale, all tensions and worries leave your body and go back into the universe where they dissolve and blend into the pure life force.

Tighten and loosen your muscles slowly in this order:

Feet. Tighten. Loosen. Take a slow, deep breath, and exhale.
Calves. Tighten. Loosen. Take a slow, deep breath, and exhale.
Thighs. Tighten. Loosen. Take a slow, deep breath, and exhale.
Hips and buttocks. Tighten. Loosen. Take a slow, deep breath, and exhale.
Stomach. Tighten. Loosen. Take a slow, deep breath, and exhale.
Back. Tighten. Loosen. Take a slow, deep breath, and exhale.
Arms. Tighten. Loosen. Take a slow, deep breath, and exhale.
Hands. Tighten. Loosen. Take a slow, deep breath, and exhale.
Neck and shoulders. Tighten. Loosen. Take a slow, deep breath, and exhale.
Face. Tighten. Loosen. Take a slow, deep breath, and exhale.

Then completely relax and take eight more, deep slow breaths. Inhale the universal life energy through your nose and exhale tension through your mouth.

Set the intent: *Whoever I am, whatever I am, whatever I need, whatever is right for me—so be it. I open to insight. I open to receive.*

Now that you are completely relaxed, give yourself over to the music. Focus inward to your vast self, as vast as the universe. Journey within. Envision yourself as an abandoned child alone and neglected because of what you have done to psychologically or physically survive. This is the part of yourself that you or others have beaten up. The part of you that feels guilty and unworthy. See yourself ragged and lonely, having endured much. Take back this part of yourself. Bring this beat up child out of the harsh elements. Nurture the child with food, warmth, and love. Embrace the child. Send understanding and forgiveness from your heart into the child's heart. Tell the child, "No matter what you've said or done, or what anyone else has said or done to you, you are still a valuable person."

As the music ends, absorb the child into your heart. Rest a few moments and bask in this forgiveness.

Record your experience.

_____

_____

_____

_____

_____

_____

_____

_____

_____

_____

_____

_____

Draw a picture or symbol that summarizes the experience.

Create a key phrase that summarizes this experience. Example: "I love and forgive myself."

_____

When needed, say the mantra silently, and visualize the picture or symbol. This will generate a peaceful, empowered, and clear state of mind.

Δ

Gem of Wisdom
Deaf and dumb the dragon is
to its victim's plea—
Aye, I am the victim
And aye, the dragon's me!

Live the Mystery

Date_____

5

WORKSHOP FIVE
MEETING YOUR DEEP DOWN NEEDS

Our deep down needs are often clouded with surface needs. *I want a romantic partner,* often shrouds the deeper need of, *I want to be loved.* Hence, it is confusing sometimes to identify our deep down needs. If we cannot do that, we often try to meet our needs in ways that are less satisfactory than if we had a better understanding of what would truly fulfill us.

The following exercise is designed to extract the root of our need, rather than what seems apparent. *I need money* might really be, *I need the security of shelter and food.*

Describe the ideal place and the ideal home in which you would like to live—actual or fictional. Money is not an issue. See the scenery, feel the energy of the area. See your home. You can embellish it with food, furniture, hobby supplies, entertainment systems, or an office to work. Choose if want a companion, family, or neighbors, and who they might be. Describe this place and your living situation in detail.

_____

_____

_____

_____

_____

_____

_____

_____

_____

_____

_____

_____

What needs might be met by living in this special place? Examples: solitude, financial security, time to play, companionship, need for nature, a great place to hike.

_____

_____

_____

_____

_____

_____

Etch this place in your mind. Know that you can go there anytime within yourself.

Other than food and shelter, list your top ten needs. Examples: love, safety, money, animals, wisdom, patience, friends, a lover, a mate, children, a hobby, nature, night life, autonomy, a job, a new career, adventure, a car, a new wardrobe, hibernation to think and heal, notoriety, success in relationships, career success, an education, a vacation, inner development, courage, to be left alone, confidence, or any other needs that come to mind.

1._____   6. _____

2._____   7._____

3._____   8._____

4._____   9._____

5._____   10. _____

Now that you have listed your top ten needs, look beneath the obvious, and uncover what it is that you *really* need. Example: the *need for a lover* might really be about the *need to be touched*. The *need to be thin* might really be about *gaining approval*. The need for a pet might really be about the *need to take care of something*. You might have more than one answer for each need. Example: *The need for money is really about security and freedom.*

In the exercise below, state what each need (that you have listed above) is really about. If you accomplished this in the original exercise, restate your answer.

1. Need #1 is really about _____.

2. Need #2 is really about _____.

3. Need #3 is really about _____.

4. Need #4 is really about _____.

5. Need #5 is really about _____.

6. Need #6 is really about _____.

7. Need #7 is really about _____.

8. Need #8 is really about _____.

9. Need #9 is really about _____.

10. Need #10 is really about _____.

Now summarize the essence of your needs. Examples: love, security, touch, confidence.

What I really need is _____

_____

_____

_____.

We often feel that our needs can only be met if we can get others to comply. Yet, often, when we begin to give *ourselves* what we need, others do comply. Taking steps to meet your own needs will attract others into your life in a positive way. Think of some ways that you can meet your needs. Examples: *When I need excitement, instead of being upset that no one will do anything with me, I could join a travel group. Or, when I need to feel loved, instead of pining, I could be pamper myself at a spa. Or, when I need friends, instead of sitting in my room, I can volunteer in an area that interests me.*

State ways in which you can meet your own needs.

1. *When I need _____

instead of _____

I could _____.

2. *When I need _____

instead of _____

I could _____.

3. *When I need _____

instead of _____

I could _____.

4. *When I need _____

instead of _____

I could _____.

5. *When I need _____

instead of _____

I could _____.

When we begin to meet our own needs, others will begin to treat us the way we treat ourselves.

Healing and Balancing Exercise for Quenching Needs. We all have healing ability—use it on yourself.

> **Place one hand at the base of your breastbone.**
> **Place the other hand on your forehead.**
> **Concentrate deeply. Repeat silently, or aloud, for at least two minutes,**
> **"I balance myself to meet my needs."**

Your state of mind begins to change, and you know your deep down needs will be met in a way that is truly right for you.

Relaxation and Creative Visualization Exercise.

Lie in a comfortable position. Play instrumental music that makes you feel good: classical, new age, or music that is gentle, sweeping, or of dynamic beauty. As music is plays, close your eyes. Inhale through your nose, and exhale through your mouth slowly, eight times. Visualize that you are inhaling the power of the universe, which purifies and attunes you physically, emotionally, mentally, and metaphysically. When you exhale, all the tensions and worries leave your body and go back into the universe where they dissolve and blend into the pure life force.

Tighten and loosen your muscles slowly in this order.

Feet. Tighten. Loosen. Take a slow, deep breath, and exhale.
Calves. Tighten. Loosen. Take a slow, deep breath, and exhale.
Thighs. Tighten. Loosen. Take a slow, deep breath, and exhale.
Hips and buttocks. Tighten. Loosen. Take a slow, deep breath, and exhale.
Stomach. Tighten. Loosen. Take a slow, deep breath, and exhale.
Back. Tighten. Loosen. Take a slow, deep breath, and exhale.
Arms. Tighten. Loosen. Take a slow, deep breath, and exhale.
Hands. Tighten. Loosen. Take a slow, deep breath, and exhale.
Neck and shoulders. Tighten. Loosen. Take a slow, deep breath, and exhale.
Face. Tighten. Loosen. Take a slow, deep breath, and exhale.

Then completely relax and take eight more slow, deep breaths. Inhale the universal life energy through your nose and exhale tension through your mouth.

Set the intent: *Whoever I am, whatever I am, whatever I need, whatever is right for me—so be it. I open to insight. I open to receive.*

Now that you are completely relaxed, give yourself over to the music. Focus inward to your vast self, as vast as the universe. Journey within. As the music plays, be in your special place. Call with your mind and heart for the *essence* of all you need, thereby clarifying what is missing in your life. Release the idea about the *manner* in which you wish your needs to be met. Instead of calling for a mate (you might get one and not like the experience) call to feel loved. This will bring you the most amazing and unexpected experiences. Instead of calling for increased finances, call for security and freedom. Again, this will yield the most amazing and unexpected experiences. Let the energy be pure and release expectations. Know that what is truly right for you *beyond* your conscious analysis—will manifest. Thoughts and feelings are energy. Shining these energies with a pure call from your heart will manifest what you truly need to feed your being. After calling out, be still, and quiet: free of thoughts, empty like a vase, hollow like a reed. Listen, feel, experience.

After this, you might want to turn down or turn off the volume on the music to perform a chant. Often, chanting is best done with no competing music in the background, but it is important that you do what feels best for you. Chant out loud, the following: *All I truly am and need becomes the flower from the seed.* Give yourself to the chant. You might talk louder, or softer, or catch a rhythm. Allow the chant to encompass you. Do not get caught up in how many times you say it. Vocalizing has a healing effect, so saying it out loud carries importance. Don't stop the chant until it naturally fades into silence.

When you are done, know that the essence of what you *truly* need is in the process of manifesting in your life. Rest a few moments and bask in the experience.

Record your experience.

_____

_____

_____

_____

_____

_____

_____

_____

_____

_____

_____

_____

_____

_____

Draw a picture or symbol that summarizes your experience.

Create a key phrase that summarizes this experience. Example: "What I give to myself will come my way."

_____

When needed, say the mantra silently, and visualize the picture or symbol. This will generate a peaceful, empowered, and clear state of mind.

Δ

Gem of Wisdom
Like all great mysteries
you too are a mystery,
a boundless, timeless, ageless being,
ever being discovered and experienced.

Live the Mystery

WORKSHOP SIX
GOING TO THE ROOT

Various events occur in everyone's life. These events and our reactions to them help shape the course of our lifetime. Like a stone thrown in a pond, ripples are forthcoming, sometimes years into the future. Some events affect us so deeply that we develop behaviors, (such as sexual promiscuity or impudence, abusiveness, chronic victimization) and ideas (such as men are bad, women are evil, I am worthless) that lead us into territories (substance abuse, mental institutions, incarceration) that we'd prefer not to experience. One might question, how did this happen? How did I get here? Understanding and healing the roots of those behaviors can free us from ways of thinking that inhibit or stress our current life experience. **If you are currently in therapy, it is advised you consult with your therapist regarding before proceeding with this workshop.**

State a disturbing event in your life.

_____

What conclusions did you draw about life because of this event? Examples: *Life is hard. It doesn't pay to be nice.*

_____

_____

_____

What conclusions did you draw about yourself because of this event? Examples: *I am weak. I trust too easily. It is my fault that this happened to me. I do not measure up.*

_____

_____

_____

What negative behaviors have you developed as a result of this event? Examples: *I hardly ever go outside. I ward off any possible romantic relationship. Substance abuse. I cry a lot. I am mad all the time. I distract myself by gambling.*

_____

_____

_____

Because of this event, I have issues with _____

_____

_____.

Sometimes we can take a disturbing event, and find ways to grow. If you have developed any positive behaviors as a result of this event, list them below. Examples: _I learned self-defense. I went into counseling. I learned how to meditate._

_____

_____

We are affected by what happens to us. However, _what we do with what happens to us_ can quite literally change our life course.

At the root of our psychological wounds, our sense of worth has been threatened, producing conscious or unconscious anger, sadness, depression, fear, guilt, and anxiety. These unpleasant emotions are less from the events that seemingly produced them, and more from the conclusions drawn at the time about one's self, others, and life. These conclusions are often carried far into the future, profoundly affecting behavior and major life decisions.

There is an equation that determines what conclusions we will draw. This equation is comprised of multiple factors, so numerous we are usually not even aware of them all. Age, circumstance, time of year, our personality, the personalities of the other people present at the event, fears one had at that time, and multiple other circumstances. The conclusions one draws from an impacting event are made at that _very moment_.

The conclusions drawn are at least in some way skewed due to lack of understanding the whole picture. Like seeds, by watering these conclusions, there sprouts an almost fictitious explanation of who we are, why we are, and our choice of psychological survival.

Example: Your mom gave you up for adoption. You conclude that you must not be too worthy. You are angry that your bad mom could throw you away. You move into life with a fear of abandonment and are hard pressed to foster any meaningful relationship. In this case, consider this: Maybe your biological mom lived in poverty with other children to care for, abandoned by her husband, and no support system. Maybe she gave you away so that you could have a life that she never did. Or, maybe she was a drug addict, fearing for your safety because she felt controlled by her addiction. Maybe, she gave you up for adoption out of love. Or, maybe she just knew that having a baby at that time in her life was more than she could handle, but she refused to abort you. Maybe she fought for your life, and cried every day that you were in her womb, knowing she must give you up for adoption. And yet, no matter what the case, a myriad of conclusions can be drawn that facilitate behaviors and influence future decisions.

The mother who gives up the baby, too is left to carry conclusions for her decision. *I am a bad person for giving up my child. I don't deserve happiness because I am a bad person. Good things should not happen to me. I know I am no good. I will settle for crumbs thrown my way because I should be punished.* The mother too, lives her life based on the conclusions she drew from the event of giving her child up for adoption.

If every human is fueled by skewed conclusions drawn from various events, imagine how many dramas are incited by bunches of us interacting with each other. A favorite drama often has blame as the star of the show. We love to blame each other, or at least ourselves. Not only does it create drama, it also incapacities us to improve our lives.

These conclusions begin from the moment we are born, and ripple outward, often until the day we die. However, consider this: Each generation deals with harsh life events, the results of which inevitably pass to the next generation. Our thoughts, feelings, and behaviors are influenced by our upbringing, and the way others treat us. We might repeat how we were raised, or do to others what they did to us, with our own children or with other people. We might make small improvements, or rebel and go to the opposite extreme with our parenting technique, or make sure that what happened to us, happens to no other. Even if we don't reproduce, we have still been influenced by those who raised us. And those who treated us badly were influenced by those who raised them, going back thousands of years. Given this, is there really any fault? Or is everyone, even those to whom we are not related, just reacting to *their* upbringing and doing the best they can?

There will always be someone to blame, and nothing changes. The most effective halting of a negative ripple and the beginnings of a more constructive ripple that will echo out into future generations, involves embracing our worth no matter what happened to us, embrace it deep, embrace it with pure heart, and don't look back.

It might seem simplistic to merely embrace yourself, and believe that somehow the pain will diminish. However, the state of mind to be kind and loving to yourself, to believe in yourself, that somehow you have what it takes to overcome, heal, and grow—is highly powerful.

This is a decision that you make, and only you can make it. Either you decide to hold onto the pain, or you decide to let it go. Make a statement below.

If I hold onto the pain, then _____

_____

_____.

If I release the pain, then_____

_____

_____.

Every harsh event yields a gift. It is up to us to find it. Example: *I was beaten as a child— therefore, my children are raised using natural and logical consequence, never violence, not even a spanking.* Example: *I was mugged, but it brought me into counseling, and I learned so much about myself, and improved my overall life.*

What gift did you receive from your disturbing life event, or what gift can you receive, if only you will allow?

_____

_____

_____.

State a new set of constructive conclusions from the old event. Example: **Even though** my mom abandoned me at birth, **I am** worthwhile and ... **I have** a lot to offer the world and ... **My life** presented many challenges that made me a really strong person.

Even though _____

I am_____

_____.

I have _____

_____.

My life _____

_____.

Healing and Balancing Exercise for Self-Embrace. We all have healing energies. Use them on yourself.

> **Place one hand at the base of your breastbone.**
> **Place the other hand over your heart.**
> **Concentrate deeply. Repeat to yourself or aloud for at least two minutes, "I matter!"**

Loving, healing energy has been generated inside you, and you feel much better.

Relaxation and Creative Visualization Exercise.

Lie in a comfortable position. Play instrumental music that makes you feel good: classical, new age, or music that is gentle, sweeping, or of dynamic beauty. When the music is playing, close your eyes. Inhale through your nose, and exhale through your mouth slowly, eight times. Visualize that you are inhaling the power of the universe, which purifies and attunes you physically, emotionally, mentally, and metaphysically. When you exhale, all the tensions and worries leave your body and go back into the universe where they dissolve and blend into the pure life force.

Tighten and loosen your muscles slowly in this order.

Feet. Tighten. Loosen. Take a slow, deep breath, and exhale.
Calves. Tighten. Loosen. Take a slow, deep breath, and exhale.
Thighs. Tighten. Loosen. Take a slow, deep breath, and exhale.
Hips and buttocks. Tighten. Loosen. Take a slow, deep breath, and exhale.
Stomach. Tighten. Loosen. Take a slow, deep breath, and exhale.
Back. Tighten. Loosen. Take a slow, deep breath, and exhale.
Arms. Tighten. Loosen. Take a slow, deep breath, and exhale.
Hands. Tighten. Loosen. Take a slow, deep breath, and exhale.
Neck and shoulders. Tighten. Loosen. Take a slow, deep breath, and exhale.
Face. Tighten. Loosen. Take a slow, deep breath, and exhale.

Then completely relax and take eight more slow, deep breaths. Inhale the universal life energy through your nose, exhale tension through your mouth.

Set the intent: *Whoever I am, whatever I am, whatever I need, whatever is right for me—so be it. I open to insight. I open to receive.*

Now that you are completely relaxed, give yourself over to the music that is playing. Focus inward to your vast self, as vast as the universe. Journey within. Briefly think of the disturbing life event that you stated earlier. Only this time, see the event in the backdrop of a tropical beach. You absorb the healing energy of sand and surf, the blue warm sky, the breeze upon your face. Take note of the conclusions you drew about yourself. Example: *My parents hate me. I am stupid. I don't matter.* Replace them with healthy conclusions. *I am worthy. I am beautiful. I am valid.* Take a walk on the beach, and repeat the healthy conclusions over and over. Decide that you have suffered enough, and this moment, your life begins anew.

As the music ends, embrace your new conclusions and commit to using them often in your daily life. Rest a few moments, and bask in the experience.

Record your experience.

_____

_____

_____

_____

_____

_____

_____

_____

_____

_____

_____

Draw a picture or symbol that summarizes your experience.

Create a key phrase that summarizes this experience.

_____

When needed, say the mantra silently, and visualize the picture or symbol. This will generate a peaceful, empowered, and clear state of mind.

Δ

Gem of Wisdom
You can't hold onto anything,
but you can experience the flow of everything—
the full rainbow, the greater picture.
Hence, when holding on hurts you, let go.
Let the river run, and it will take you into vastness
beyond all your hopes and dreams
into an expanded perception
and an expanded experience of reality.

Live the Mystery

Date_____

WORKSHOP SEVEN
RESCUING SELF FROM THE PAST

Our current thoughts, feelings, and behaviors are generally residuals from of our past. However, our present reality is often affected because we have not discerned the difference between thoughts and feelings born from past events, and perhaps what thoughts and feelings are more appropriate for today.

This workshop is designed to bring awareness to outdated thoughts, feelings, and behaviors that might still play a significant part in your life—and yet, are no longer in your own best interest. Example: A defensive attitude toward all possible romantic partners might only have been the result of one relationship long ago. Because of this, future romances are hard pressed to blossom.

Before we can 'update' ourselves, in much the same manner that we would update old files, we must first find out where in the past we might yet be stuck. When that is discerned, it is a matter of deleting thoughts and feelings that no longer work for us, and entering new data, that does.

Whether we can initially see it or not, there is almost always some sort of negative influence that our parents or guardians had on us. This does not mean our parents or guardians are, or were bad people. They are, or were merely—human, just as their parents or guardians were merely human. People in general do not set out to cause harm. And if they do, they often don't realize it, or they believe they are doing it for the child's own good, or because they are so damaged within, they cannot stop perpetuating injury.

The following exercise will highlight adopted ways of thinking by those who raised us. Sometimes, what we have adopted is compatible with who we truly are. Sometimes, it is not. If we are living someone else's code of life and it is not addressing our unique needs, depression or anxiety can set in. A component in retrieving personal power lies in becoming aware of how our thinking might be a product of others. When we can finally feel what we *want to feel*, rather than how we *do feel*, we have freed ourselves from the residuals of difficult times past.

What demeaning statements do you most remember your mother or guardian saying? Examples: *You are a slob. You are lazy. Put on a smile, even if you're hurting inside.*

1. _____

2. _____

3. _____

4. _____

In what way do you think these statements may have influenced your thoughts and feelings about yourself?

_____

_____

_____.

What demeaning statements do you most remember your father or guardian saying? Examples: *Don't be a cry baby. You don't use your head.*

1. _____

2. _____

3. _____

4. _____

In what way do you think these statements may have influenced your thoughts and feelings about yourself?

_____

_____

_____.

This next exercise involves putting a positive spin on the very 'slams' that have affected you to this day. Think of the negative statements and create some new statements that are more constructive for you. Examples: *Okay, so I am messy. Messiness is often a mark of highly creative people. Okay, so I carry some weight. Round people can be most lovely. Okay, so I didn't get good grades. There are qualities more important like having a good heart. Okay, so I got into a lot of trouble as a kid, which just proves I have an adventurous spirit. Okay, so I ran away from home a lot, which means I have a strong will to survive. Okay, so my mom always called me selfish, but it was only so that I would continue to be her 'assistant mom,' which proves I was not selfish at all.* Take time to think about this. It is easy to forget or to be in denial.

1. Okay, so _____

Positive spin_____

_____.

2. Okay, so _____

Positive spin_____

_____.

3. Okay, so _____

Positive spin_____

_____.

4. Okay, so _____

Positive spin_____

_____.

5. Okay, so _____

Positive spin_____

_____.

6. Okay, so _____

Positive spin_____

_____.

7. Okay, so _____

Positive spin_____

_____.

8. Okay, so _____

Positive spin_____

_____.

Sometimes we get so caught up in the negatives of our childhood, that we forget the positives. List the positive influences your parents or guardians may have had on you. If it is difficult to pull them out of a negative past, look harder. Example: *My mom always criticized me, but that gave me a sense of defiance that has helped me to be my own person today.* Example: *My dad always seemed mean, but on holidays his warmth did come out. I guess that is why I am so warm on holidays.* Or perhaps, you remember many wonderful influences your parents or guardians had on you, and this exercise will prove less challenging, yet generate even more warm and positive feelings toward those who raised you.

My mom (or guardian) . . .

1. *My mom (or guardian) _____

_____.

Because of that I _____

_____.

2. *My mom (or guardian) _____

_____.

Because of that I _____

_____.

3. *My mom (or guardian) _____

_____.

Because of that I _____

_____.

My dad (or guardian) . . .

1. *My dad (or guardian) _____

_____.

Because of that I _____

_____.

2. *My dad (or guardian) _____

_____.

Because of that I _____

_____.

3. *My dad (or guardian) _____

_____.

Because of that I _____

_____ .

You have received many gifts hidden in hardship. As you extract these gifts from your past, you can keep what helped you and shed what demeaned you. Whatever demeaned you has absolutely no bearing on your worth as a human, nor must it influence how you currently view yourself. Example: Highly creative people are often not the most organized people, because focusing on organization detracts from the spontaneity and deep concentration required for many to be creative. Oh, what great creative works would we not have today, if those with creative natures chucked it all just to keep a well-organized house and life. And what would we do without highly organized people who might seem too rigid to creative types. Utter chaos would ensue. We all carry our own special value. Being true to that, not only helps you, but the world.

Within us all is a core self that in its pure state, is beyond influence. Focus there. Focus on that. You will find yourself flowering and seeing a new spin on the negatives of 'what was.' Who you are is sacred and beautiful—as is, no matter whatever happened to you. No person outside us can taint our worth. It is only we who have perceptions of our worth being tainted, but it *never* is. Trust yourself. Love yourself. And give yourself what you need to blossom into your full potential.

Now that you might be clearer on how your past has affected your present, the following exercise will help you capture what is more compatible with the life experience you currently seek.

What is your favorite fairytale or fiction story? Example: *The Mermaid*

_____

What about this story *most* appeals to you? Example: *I love it that the mermaid is different from others and can freely swim about the ocean and be herself.*

_____

_____

_____

What feeling in you does this story evoke? Example: *The feeling of freedom.*

_____

What can you do in your life today to generate this feeling? Example: *I could give myself more time to play. I could also let others know what is important to me, and make the time to do what I love to do.*

1. _____

2. _____

3. _____

4. _____

5. _____

By keeping focus on what is important to you, rather than on what you have been *influenced to believe* is important, you can stop reacting to your present as if it were your past. Example: Your friend calls you selfish. Your mom always called you selfish, and it really upset you. You know now that taking care of yourself is not selfish. You *know* that. You embrace your worth, *now*. You need not have a negative reaction. You can smile and say, "Thanks," thinking, *I am taking care of myself, and that is good.*

Healing and Balancing Exercise for Releasing the Past. We all have healing ability—use it on yourself.

> **Place one palm over the other, resting over your heart.**
> **Concentrate deeply. Repeat silently or aloud for at least two minutes,**
> **"I am me, today, and that's okay."**

You have released yourself from the past, and accepted who you are, all that you are, this moment in time.

Relaxation and Creative Visualization Exercise.

Lie in a comfortable position. Play instrumental music that makes you feel good: classical, new age, or music with gentle, sweeping, or of dynamic beauty. When the music is playing, close your eyes. Inhale through your nose, and exhale through your mouth slowly, eight times. Visualize that you are inhaling the power of the universe, which purifies and attunes you physically, emotionally, mentally, and metaphysically. When you exhale, all the tensions and worries leave your body and go back into the universe where they dissolve and blend into the pure life force.

Tighten and loosen your muscles slowly in this order.

Feet. Tighten. Loosen. Take a slow, deep breath, and exhale.
Calves. Tighten. Loosen. Take a slow, deep breath, and exhale.
Thighs. Tighten. Loosen. Take a slow, deep breath, and exhale.
Hips and buttocks. Tighten. Loosen. Take a slow, deep breath, and exhale.
Stomach. Tighten. Loosen. Take a slow, deep breath, and exhale.
Back. Tighten. Loosen. Take a slow, deep breath, and exhale.
Arms. Tighten. Loosen. Take a slow, deep breath, and exhale.
Hands. Tighten. Loosen. Take a slow, deep breath, and exhale.
Neck and shoulders. Tighten. Loosen. Take a slow, deep breath, and exhale.
Face. Tighten. Loosen. Take a slow, deep breath, and exhale.

Then completely relax and take eight slow, deep breaths. Inhale the universal life energy through your nose and exhale tension through your mouth.

Set the intent: *Whoever I am, whatever I am, whatever I need, whatever is right for me—so be it. I open to insight. I open to receive.*

Now that you are completely relaxed, give yourself over to the music that is playing. Focus inward to your vast self, as vast as the universe. Journey within. You are moving through a tunnel. At various times you will sense an opening to the right or left where a part of you is still stuck in a past experience. Move into that opening. You will see yourself perhaps at a certain age, caught up somehow. Example: You see yourself at age five, so shy that you never play with anyone. Take the five year old, and bring that part of you back into the main tunnel. Move deeper into the tunnel (you, and the freed part of you). Each time you sense a part of you trapped in the past, go into the opening and free that part, until all your past selves are freed. Then the group of you (you and your past selves) begin to fly. You move deeper into the tunnel. You all come out into the universe and blend into one being whereupon you soar amongst the beautiful stars! You feel bright, refreshed, rejuvenated, and freed.

When the music ends, you know you can live fully in the present, free of the past. Rest a few moments and bask in the experience.

Record your experience.

_____

_____

_____

_____

_____

_____

_____

_____

_____

_____

_____

_____

_____

_____

_____

_____

_____

Draw a picture or symbol that summarizes your experience.

Create a key phrase that summarizes this experience.

_____

When needed, say the mantra silently, and visualize the picture or symbol. This will generate a peaceful, empowered, and clear state of mind.

Δ

Gem of Wisdom
It's not what happens to you.
It's what you do with what happens to you.
Every hardship is a gift, if only you will embrace it.
Life is fair—eventually.

Live the Mystery

Date_____

8

WORKSHOP EIGHT
POSITIVE RELATIONS WITH SIGNIFICANT OTHERS: LISTENING

The biggest source of tension between significant others is the lack of respect for the other person's individuality, or the other person's lack of respect for our individuality. As humans, we have tendencies to want others to behave in the ways that serve us best, or we are coerced into becoming what will best serve others.

Avoiding or breaking these negative ways of relating, requires awareness of the following:

1. People, in general, *like* to make each other happy. This is a wonderful human quality. We have the ability to 'feel' for each other. However, it is no one's *job* to make us happy, and it is not our *job* to make others happy. We are responsible for our own happiness, and others are responsible for theirs. Making another happy should be compatible with being true to one's self.
2. Express true feelings, such as *I feel hurt and disrespected*, instead of casting blame or throwing insults such as *I hate you! You are so mean!* (This will be discussed further in Workshop Nine).
3. Respect the views of others even when we don't agree.
4. When others are speaking, take time to really hear what they are saying, instead of cutting them off with our viewpoint. Let them know that we understand by summarizing what they seem to be expressing. When that is done, we can then express our views. This will be further discussed in this workshop.
5. Give to ourselves what we are trying to get from others (security, raised self-esteem etc.).
6. Release the need to control those around us. Instead, take action to improve our lives. Regarding children, the goal is to provide a structured environment to help them learn and grow in a nurturing way, supported by natural and logical consequences. This is not the same as control. Example: Your child won't come to the dinner table. Eat dinner. Clear the table. When your child comes into the kitchen for food, the response is, "Oh, you missed dinner. Here are some healthy snacks to tide you over until breakfast." The child will not likely miss dinner again, and the parent didn't have to suffer trying to get the child to the table.
7. When making family decisions, let everyone's thoughts and feelings be heard, including our own. Ascertain whose needs are greater at any given time to determine solutions. Sometimes, with the creative input of everyone, not yet thought of solutions may occur to satisfy everyone's needs without anyone sacrificing. Consistently reevaluate the family's needs as time goes by.
8. Let our decisions on how to behave with significant others be led by what 'feels' right deep down inside, not by what we *should or should not do*, or by the influence of the outside world's view of 'our' situation. We are the only ones in the heart of our situation, and we are the best candidates to make ultimate decisions.

To improve all relations with significant others, effective listening is imperative. Often what drives people to counseling is simply a need to be heard. And often what strengthens a relationship is knowing that we *are* heard.

Listening Exercises

Effective listening involves hearing what a person is saying, as well as responding to what a person is doing. Words and behavior are significant cues to what is going on with our significant others.

A significant other screams, "I don't ever want to see you again!"
What would be a typical response?

_____

The most productive response is a summarization of your significant other's *words*. An effective listening response to, "I don't ever want to see you again!" might be, "You sound like you are sick of me."

A significant other is moping around the house. What would be a typical response to this *behavior?*

_____

The most productive response is a summary of your significant other's *behavior*. An effective summary response to a significant other moping around the house might me, "You seem upset."

This method will extract what is really going on with the other person. If you continue listening effectively, those you listen to might even discover more about themselves. Often the root of problems can be found this way, and then solved. The challenge is to refrain from a defensive, offensive, or rescuing mode by anything the person says or does. Just . . . listen, and respond in summary.

To practice summarizing another's behavior or words, think of an isolated behavior, or comment (positive or negative) of a significant other (child, sibling, spouse etc.). List it and then practice writing a sentence to reflect the behavior or words. You will have four opportunities to practice.

Example: Significant other's words: "Go away, I don't want you around."
Summary sentence: "You seem angry with me, and you want me gone."

Example: Significant other's behavior: Your child pretends not to hear you.
Summary sentence: "You seem to be ignoring me."

*Incident 1. Significant other's behavior or words.

_____

Summary sentence.

_____.

*Incident 2. Significant other's behavior or words.

_____

Summary sentence.

_____.

*Incident 3. Significant other's behavior or words.

_____

Summary sentence.

_____.

*Incident 4. Significant other's behavior or words.

_____

Summary sentence.

_____.

Continue to summarize whatever your significant other says until the thoughts and feelings are expressed. The conversation may or may not go far. Don't push it. Your real message is _I am here, and I will listen._ Once your significant other knows that he or she can open up and communicate with you without being attacked, and actually be heard—then constructive communication is imminent.

An example of an ongoing effective listening conversation might go like this:

Behavior: Your significant other seems to be ignoring you.

You: "You seem to be ignoring me."
Significant Other: "I _am_ ignoring you."
You: "So, you don't want anything to do with me."
Significant Other: "No, I hate you right now."
You: "So, you are mad at me."
Significant Other: "Yes, you embarrassed me at the party."
You: "So, you are mad at me because I embarrassed you."
Significant Other: "Yes, you never think about my feelings."
You: "You think I am insensitive to you."
Significant Other: "Well, not all the time, but in public, yes."
You: "So in public, you think I should be more sensitive to your feelings."

Significant Other: "Yes, it would mean a lot to me if you would do that."
You: "If I do that, then you will feel better?"
Significant Other: "Yes, if you do that, I will feel better."

In this example, the significant other feels heard, and the beginnings of effective communication foster an improved relationship.

Now it's your turn. Think of a time when a significant other was upset. Create a fictional conversation. Respond with respect in an effort to truly understand what is going on with that person. Stay on track summarizing the responses without getting defensive, offense, or asking questions. The goal is to get the other person to open up, not clam up. Write the behavior or initial words below. Examples: *Your child hits the wall angrily. Your mate is sitting alone in the dark, looking sad. Your friend is glaring at you.* Your mate says, *You can be so dumb, sometimes.* Your friend says, *You don't care about me at all.*

Behavior or initial words _____

Your Response: _____

_____.

Significant Other: _____

_____.

Your Response: _____

_____.

Significant Other: _____

_____.

Your Response: _____

_____.

Significant Other: _____

_____.

Your Response: _____

_____.

Significant Other_____

_____.

Your Response: _____

_____.

Significant Other: _____

_____.

Your Response: _____

_____.

Significant Other: _____

_____.

Your Response: _____

_____.

Review your answers. Make sure you didn't respond defensively, offensively, ask questions, or add information that the speaker did not give. Practice this with others. When you listen without judgment, the most beautiful bridges can occur between two people. After the listening is done, the conversation can progress into a meaningful discussion.

Healing and Balancing Exercise for Respecting Others. We all have healing ability—use it on yourself.

> **Place one palm over the other,**
> **and place both at the base of your breastbone.**
> **Concentrate deeply. Repeat silently or aloud for at least two minutes,**
> **"My worth is secure, no matter what others have to say."**

Now, no matter what anyone else might communicate to you, your self-worth will not be assaulted.

Relaxation and Creative Visualization Exercise.
Lie in a comfortable position. Play instrumental music that makes you feel good: classical, new age, or music that is gentle, sweeping, or of dynamic beauty. When the music is playing, close your eyes. Inhale through your nose and exhale through your mouth slowly, eight times. Visualize that you are inhaling the power of the universe, which purifies and attunes you physically, emotionally, mentally, and metaphysically. When you exhale, all the tensions and worries leave your body and go back into the universe where they dissolve and blend into the pure life force.

Tighten and loosen your muscles slowly in this order.

Feet. Tighten. Loosen. Take a slow, deep breath, and exhale.

Calves. Tighten. Loosen. Take a slow, deep breath, and exhale.
Thighs. Tighten. Loosen. Take a slow, deep breath, and exhale.
Hips and buttocks. Tighten. Loosen. Take a slow, deep breath, and exhale.
Stomach. Tighten. Loosen. Take a slow, deep breath, and exhale.
Back. Tighten. Loosen. Take a slow, deep breath, and exhale.
Arms. Tighten. Loosen. Take a slow, deep breath, and exhale.
Hands. Tighten. Loosen. Take a slow, deep breath, and exhale.
Neck and shoulders. Tighten. Loosen. Take a slow, deep breath, and exhale.
Face. Tighten. Loosen. Take a slow, deep breath, and exhale.

Then completely relax and take eight more slow, deep breaths. Inhale the universal life energy through your nose and exhale tension through your mouth.

Set the intent: *Whoever I am, whatever I am, whatever I need, whatever is right for me—so be it. I open to insight. I open to receive.*

Now that you are completely relaxed, give yourself over to the music that is playing. Focus inward to your vast self, as vast as the universe. Journey within. You come upon the part of yourself that does not feel heard, frustration on face, body dejected. Move inside this part of yourself. Be the unheard person. Imagine that the best listener in the world is before you. Express yourself to this great listener, whatever it is that you need to say. Let your thoughts and feelings pour out. It is okay to talk out loud if it helps. Maybe you need to reveal some things about yourself. Or, maybe others just can't hear or understand you. Try again, now. Keep talking until you feel a catharsis. When you are done, you notice that this great listener is actually the wise sage inside yourself. Your wise sage embraces your expressive self. Soak in this self-acceptance. You have validated your own thoughts and feelings without judgment. Feeling truly heard, you can now easily and patiently listen to others in your life. Acknowledge that you hear them. Release judgment. Open to understanding.

As the music ends, you feel heard and respected and you are willing to hear and respect others. Rest a few moments and bask in the experience.

Record your experience.

_____

_____

_____

_____

_____

_____

_____

_____

_____

_____

_____

_____

_____

_____

Draw a picture or symbol that summarizes your experience.

Create a key phrase that summarizes this experience.

_____

Whenever needed, say the mantra silently, and visualize the picture or symbol. This will generate a peaceful, empowered, and clear state of mind.

Δ

Gem of Wisdom
The only person you can change is yourself.
Change your response to others and they will change their response to you.

Live the Mystery

9

WORKSHOPS NINE
POSITIVE RELATIONS WITH SIGNFICANT OTHERS: SELF EXPRESSION

Healthy self-expression is often hard to do. Our world is filled with the multifaceted opinions of others and we are constantly judged. Our personal lives are subject to the needs and issues of our significant others. Sometimes, it is easier to repress our more uncomfortable feelings. Sometimes, if we repress them too long, they burst out in manners that exacerbate an already negative situation, or in ways that hurt us. Healthy self-expression always involves sharing your own experience with another without blaming them or yourself. It is a statement of fact.

Components of Healthy Self-Expression

State the Situation: "When you come home late . . ."
Insert an emotion: "I feel angry. . ."
Tell why you feel, what you feel, without blaming: "—because I have issues with trust."

A non-judgmental statement like this creates a bridge of understanding between two people. What often keeps us from building that bridge is the notion that we must uphold the image of being perfect in order to be loved, or we like to pretend that we *are* perfect to avoid dealing with deeper issues, or we don't want to expose our imperfections or vulnerabilities because we do not trust another with that information.

We might punish others by not communicating and give them the silent treatment. But then our feelings build up inside like a pressure cooker and ultimately lead to an emotional explosion or a wedge in the relationship. Practice communicating. It might take some alone time for us to understand what we are feeling in order to communicate constructively. However, relationships work best when we say what we are feeling as we experience it.

When deeply hurt or angered, it is often difficult to communicate constructively even if we know how. However, if we can take a deep breath and step forward without shame or judgment of right or wrong, and speak our truth—we will experience a kind of proclamation in who we are, a spreading of wings, so to speak. It is about communicating our reality to another. All humans have vulnerable areas and 'issues.' Our issues are no less important than anyone else's. We have a right to express ourselves and maintain self-respect even when what we share might reveal vulnerabilities within ourselves.

The following exercise is designed to help you explore your current communication style, and explore how it may have come to develop.

When you are mad at a significant other, what do you *usually* do? Example: *I repress my emotions.*

When I am mad at a significant other, I _____

_____.

When a significant other hurts your feelings, what do you *usually* do? Example: *I go into the bathroom and cry.*

When a significant other hurts my feelings, I _____

_____.

What did your mother or guardian do when she was mad? Example: *When my mother or guardian was mad, she yelled and gave a long lecture of criticism.*

When my mother or guardian was mad, she _____

_____.

What did your mother or guardian do when she was sad? Example: *When my mother or guardian was sad, she would snap and demand to be left alone.*

When my mother or guardian was sad, she _____

_____.

What did your mother or guardian do when she was afraid? Example: *When my mother or guardian was afraid, she called everyone she knew and talked for hours.*

When my mother or guardian was afraid, she _____

_____.

What did your father or guardian do when he was mad? Example: *When my father or guardian was mad, he would tell me to go to my room.*

When my father or guardian was mad, he _____

_____.

When your father or guardian was sad, what did he do? Example: *When my father or guardian was sad, he would drink alcohol.*

When my father or guardian was sad, he _____

_____.

When your father or guardian was afraid, what did he do? Example: *When my father or guardian was afraid, he yelled at everyone.*

When my father or guardian was afraid, he _____

_____.

Frequently, the ways we communicate are learned from those who raised us. Sometimes, we choose ways completely opposite to avoid repeating a past.

Circle the degree that your method of communicating reflects those who raised you.

none   a little   a lot   overwhelmingly

Communication that builds positive relations with significant others involves:

  *Intent to improve the relationship.
  *Intent to avoid misunderstandings.
  *Being honest about true feelings.
  *Courageously sharing with another.
  *Taking responsibility for feelings. (How one responds is not the fault of another, but a
    reflection of who *we* are.)
  *Don't communicate, expecting your significant other to change. (Communicate for clear
    self-expression, emotional catharsis, and out of respect for ourselves.)

If you cannot express your feelings constructively, where did that block come from? Example: *As a child, I was punished for expressing my thoughts and feelings.*

_____

_____.

If you cannot express your feelings constructively, what do you fear might happen if you did? Example: *I fear I will be judged and . . .* Example: *I fear losing the control that I have over others and . . .*

If I freely and constructively expressed my feelings, I fear_____

_____

_____.

What inside you needs expressing? Example: *I need to express my pain.*

I need to express _____.

If you knew that you could express yourself consequence free, what would you say, perhaps shout, perhaps scream? It's okay to rant. Example: *I am so tired of being taken for granted. I can't take it anymore. I feel like no one cares about me and . . .*

_____

_____

_____

_____

_____

_____.

Anger, fear, and sorrow are not bad. How we use them determines whether they work for us, or against us. Healthy self-expression will change the outcome of any situation immensely. Expressing self in a constructive way requires one to probe their inner being, so that accurate expression can be had. This next exercise will help clarify your feelings that you might be able to better communicate them later. Stretch your mind to fill in every blank. Sometimes, there are deep down, angers, fears, and sorrows in which we are not aware. This exercise can bring to light underlying feelings that can promote profound self-understanding.

ANGER

1. I feel angry when_____.

2. I feel angry when_____.

3. I feel angry when_____.

4. I feel angry when_____.

5. I feel angry when_____.

6. I feel angry when_____.

7. I feel angry when_____.

FEAR

1. I feel afraid when_____.

2. I feel afraid when_____.

3. I feel afraid when_____.

4. I feel afraid when_____.

5. I feel afraid when_____.

6. I feel afraid when_____.

7. I feel afraid when_____.

SORROW

1. I feel sad when_____.

2. I feel sad when_____.

3. I feel sad when_____.

4. I feel sad when_____.

5. I feel sad when_____.

6. I feel sad when_____.

7. I feel sad when_____.

When we feel anger, fear, or sorrow, it is usually because our self-worth has been assaulted, or our confidence in handling situations is low. Therefore, the constructive solution is to build our self-worth and confidence in our abilities—from within. Often, our emotions are reflections of our perception of a situation. *I got rejected, this means I don't measure up.* Just because we perceive something a certain way this doesn't mean it is true. Be open to the idea that *self-worth is intrinsic.* Our perceptions and conclusions of what we have done or others have done to us, does not define our worth. However, since this way of thinking takes time to manifest, communicating our sensitivities with our significant others will also, in the long run, make our lives less stressful and our relationships more meaningful.

JOY

1. I feel joy when_____.

2. I feel joy when_____.

3. I feel joy when_____.

4. I feel joy when_____.

5. I feel joy when_____.

6. I feel joy when_____.

7. I feel joy when_____.

When we feel joy, it often because either our self-worth is affirmed, we are doing something that reflects who are as an individual, as in painting, hiking, staring at a sunset, or we are happy for another. Promoting joy in our lives is often forgotten in the light of everyday life tensions. Do something each day to bring yourself joy. This promotes self-healing and positive communication with others. Expressing love and happiness is every bit as important as expressing our more unpleasant emotions.

Now it is your turn to practice constructive communication.

Examples:

1. *When you shout at me, I feel angry because I don't deserve to be treated like that.*
2. *When you tell me what to do, I resent it because I am a capable, grown-up person.*
3. *When you didn't show up, I felt disrespected because my time is important too.*

Do not say, for example: *When you take my car without asking, I feel mad because you are an inconsiderate jerk.* The term, *inconsiderate jerk* is passing judgment on the other person. When saying anything about the other person, merely describe the person's actions. Example: *When you take my car without asking, I feel angry because then I drive myself crazy trying to figure out why it is missing.* The why portion of the answer will reveal something about yourself. This might take a moment of self-probing, and in that probing, it is not uncommon to make some self-discoveries. And if the why isn't known, then the, *when you . . . I feel . . .* are often enough to get the conversation steered in a constructive direction.

Speaking this way not only effectively relays to others your experience, but it also helps clarify *to you* what your experience is really about, enabling you to understand yourself better. It is not about blame, or who is wrong or right. You feel the way you feel and that is that. Sharing who you are is a crucial step in having healthy relationships with others and more importantly, with yourself. Think of some things others have done that upset you, and fill in the blanks below, as if you are talking to that person. You will have six opportunities to practice.

*Incident 1. When you _____ ,

I feel _____ because _____

_____ .

*Incident 2. When you _____ ,

I feel _____ because _____

_____ .

*Incident 3. When you _____ ,

I feel _____ because _____

_____ .

*Incident 4. When you _____ ,

I feel _____ because _____

_____.

*Incident 5. When you _____,

I feel _____because_____

_____.

*Incident 6. When you _____,

I feel _____because_____

_____.

Sometimes we have misplaced anger, or our anger is not expressed. Example: We might scream or throw something at someone when we are hurt, instead of just saying what we feel. The situation, however, can be turned around.

Example: _When I yelled at you like that, I was feeling insecure, because what you did reminded me of all the other times that I was mistreated by others. Next time, I will try to tell you I am insecure instead of yelling._ Example: _When I threw the shoe at you, I was so angry because I didn't know how to express how truly hurt I was when you were ignoring me. Next time I will just tell you that I am hurt._

Think of a time you behaved in a manner you regret. What could you say to 'make it right?'

When you_____,

I felt_____,

because_____.

Next time _____.

Always communicate in any relationship that you value.

Healing and Balancing Exercise for Self Expression. We all have healing ability—use it on yourself.

> **Place one hand at the base of your throat.**
> **Place the other hand over your heart.**
> **Concentrate deeply. Repeat silently or aloud for at least two minutes,**
> **"Healthy self-expression is self-respect."**

It is now easy to focus on expressing your truth so that you can feel better, rather than trying to make another change.

Relaxation and Creative Visualization Exercise.

Lie in a comfortable position. Play instrumental music that makes you feel good: classical, new age, or music that is gentle, sweeping, or of dynamic beauty. When the music is playing, close your eyes. Inhale through your nose, and exhale through your mouth slowly, eight times. Visualize that you are inhaling the power of the universe, which purifies and attunes you physically, emotionally, mentally, and metaphysically. When you exhale, all the tensions and worries leave your body and go back into the universe, dissolving and blending into the pure life force.

Tighten and loosen your muscles slowly in this order.

Feet. Tighten. Loosen. Take a slow, deep breath, and exhale.
Calves. Tighten. Loosen. Take a slow, deep breath, and exhale.
Thighs. Tighten. Loosen. Take a slow, deep breath, and exhale.
Hips and buttocks. Tighten. Loosen. Take a slow, deep breath, and exhale.
Stomach. Tighten. Loosen. Take a slow, deep breath, and exhale.
Back. Tighten. Loosen. Take a slow, deep breath, and exhale.
Arms. Tighten. Loosen. Take a slow, deep breath, and exhale.
Hands. Tighten. Loosen. Take a slow, deep breath, and exhale.
Neck and shoulders. Tighten. Loosen. Take a slow, deep breath, and exhale.
Face. Tighten. Loosen. Take a slow, deep breath, and exhale.

Then completely relax and take eight slow, deep breaths. Inhale the universal life energy through your nose and exhale tension through your mouth.

Set the intent: *Whoever I am, whatever I am, whatever I need, whatever is right for me—so be it. I open to insight. I open to receive.*

Now that you are completely relaxed, give yourself over to the music that is playing. Focus inward to your vast self, as vast as the universe. Journey within. Imagine what it might feel like to constructively express yourself without expecting change from others. Imagine that by doing this, you free yourself to be who you are without shame. As the music plays, become the bird flying over landscape, gliding on the wind. You can go anywhere you like, a mountaintop, or walk on a sand beach, perch in a tree, or land next to a garden flower. The judgment of others does not affect you because you are at peace with yourself.

As the music ends, you feel at ease in expressing your truth to others.

Record your experience.

_____

_____

_____

_____

_____

_____

_____

_____

_____

_____

Draw a picture or symbol that summarizes your experience.

Create a key phrase that summarizes this experience.

_____

Whenever needed, say the mantra silently, and visualize the picture or symbol. This will generate a peaceful, empowered, and clear state of mind.

Δ
Gem of Wisdom
Everything we think and feel is valid.
Constructive self-expression is more
about taking our own pulse,
than changing the pulse of another.

Live the Mystery

10

WORKSHOP TEN
THE PHANTOM LOVER: ROMANTIC RELATIONSHIPS

Romance is popular. Romance novels abound. Humans need to feel important. In a world that can feel overwhelming, and survival is always an issue, the need to feel special to at least one person is paramount. And the need to make another special is also great. Expressing love, touch, and communion between two people—it all feels so right. Yet, numerous challenges arise from the quest for true love.

Throughout history, a common precept of the romantic relationship is two halves joining to make a whole. The idea is that people are not whole until they find their mate. This perception often leads to great conflict in the relationship, as each tends to *expect* the other to fulfill his or her needs, constantly. The idea of being one's self and being true to one's self, comes under fire when our mates expect behaviors from us that serve them, not us—and vice versa.

While there are those who have found mates highly compatible and experience a relatively peaceful relationship—more do not. Most couples have personalities somewhat in conflict, and tension cannot be avoided. Much of this comes from a misnomer of what . . . love . . . is.

We often confuse love and need. And we often use emotional blackmail to get our needs met. Imagine if we could meet most of our own needs. In other words, imagine if we could be self-actualized within the relationship. Then we would be free to truly love and support one another. We would also be free to choose when it is healthy to end a relationship, instead of remaining in a toxic situation just to have certain needs met. However, self-actualization within a relationship is rare, and exploring what lies beneath the tip of the iceberg on this topic can render great results in current or future relationships.

Most great relationships are between two self-actualized people.

Components of self-actualization.
1. Foster your uniqueness. *Allow yourself to be an individual.*
2. Heal yourself at the source of negative infliction. *Examine what ails you and take responsibility to heal your psychological wounds.*
3. Nurture yourself. *Give yourself compassion, confidence, and love.*
4. Behold your worth. *Let your actions reflect self-respect.*
5. Come into your 'own.' *Grow into your full potential.*

In order to achieve self-actualization in a romantic relationship, it is helpful to examine our ideas regarding the perfect mate.

Excluding physical attributes, what are your ideas about a perfect mate?

_____

_____

_____

_____

_____

_____

_____

_____

_____.

Have you ever known anyone who lived up to these criteria? _____

If you answered yes, put the spotlight on this person's shortcomings. Everyone has them. State these shortcomings below.

_____

_____.

Given this, did that person really fit your romantic ideal? _____

What qualities do you seek in a mate that are also characteristic of your childhood significant others (parent, sibling, relative, family friend)?

_____

_____

_____

Reviewing past and current romantic relationships, have any of your partners exhibited these qualities? If so, which qualities?

_____

_____

_____

Are there qualities that you seek in a mate that *are not* characteristic of your childhood significant others (parent, sibling, relative, family friend)?

_____

_____

_____

What *negative* qualities did your childhood significant others (parent, sibling, relative, family friend) possess?

_____

_____

_____

Reviewing past and current romantic relationships, have any of your partners exhibited these negative qualities? If so, which qualities?

_____

_____

_____

We often gravitate to what feels familiar when seeking a mate, rather than to who is truly best for us. We are comfortable with what we know (the way of a parent, sibling, etc.) and unconsciously seek to recreate it, even if it will not make us particularly happy. Open to the idea, that though perhaps uncomfortable, sometimes what feels *unfamiliar* might actually make for a better relationship.

Reviewing all past or current romantic relationships, to what degree have you chosen partners that are reminiscent of your childhood significant others (parent, sibling, relative, family friend?) Circle the appropriate answer.

none   a little   a lot   overwhelmingly

What do you expect in a current or future mate?

1. I expect my mate to _____.

2. I expect my mate to _____.

3. I expect my mate to _____.

4. I expect my mate to _____.

5. I expect my mate to _____.

6. I expect my mate to _____.

7. I expect my mate to _____.

8. I expect my mate to _____.

9. I expect my mate to _____.

10. I expect my mate to _____.

11. I expect my mate to _____.

12. I expect my mate to _____.

13. I expect my mate to _____.

14. I expect my mate to _____.

15. I expect my mate to _____.

1. I expect my mate **not to** _____.

2. I expect my mate **not to** _____.

3. I expect my mate **not to** _____.

4. I expect my mate **not to** _____.

5. I expect my mate **not to** _____.

6. I expect my mate **not to** _____.

7. I expect my mate **not to** _____.

8. I expect my mate **not to** _____.

9. I expect my mate **not to** _____.

10. I expect my mate **not to** _____.

11. I expect my mate **not to** _____.

12. I expect my mate **not to** _____.

13. I expect my mate **not to** _____.

14. I expect my mate **not to** _____.

15. I expect my mate **not to** _____.

If your mate could fulfill your every expectation, in what ways would your life be better?

_____

_____

_____

_____.

It is easier to imagine our lives bettered by having our mate or future mate fulfill all our expectations. This premise is based on another meeting all our needs. If this could be done, however, we would cease to develop into our full potential. We would not have to, because our mate would be picking up the slack. **This is not the same as a couple working as a team to enable each other to grow into their full potentials.** However, more often, couples use each other to avoid personal growth, stunting self-actualization.

Avoiding personal growth in a romantic relationship leads to a negative dependence on our mate. Example: *My mate constantly makes me feel good about myself, thus my fear of losing my mate is great. I am very clingy, and possessive, and I secretly feel nervous all the time.* Example: *My take-charge mate, who handles worldly problems for me, also tries to take charge of me, and that makes me mad. If I want my worldly problems taken care of for me, I have to put up with that.* In the first example, learning to appreciate yourself apart from your mate gives you control of your self-esteem. Therefore, no one can diminish your self-esteem, but you. Hence, the nervousness and fear, fade. In the second example: if learning how to take care of your own worldly matters (finances, insurance policies, home and car care etc.) can alleviate fear of losing or leaving a mate who takes care of that for you, it can only make you feel more capable and much safer.

Even if we could become someone else's dream mate, unless compatibility is remarkable, we would lose a measure of our individuality. If we are so busy being something for another, how can we be who we truly are? People who *give up who they are* to please their mates, experience deep unhappiness. Their worth is derived from being who their mate wants them to be, and not who they are deep down inside. This is a set up for a future emotional crisis.

This is not to say that mates cannot make an effort to fulfill each other's needs. It can be the joy of love—to give to another. It is to say, however, that *expecting* another to be a servant to our needs, and a doctor to heal our psychological wounds, is a lot to ask. Likewise, it is a lot for another to ask the same of us. When we *expect* another to give us everything we want and need, rather than *appreciating what is given* as a gift, the relationship begins to falter.

However, there are basic expectations that reflect self-respect, such as *I expect my mate not to hit me. I expect my mate to be faithful to me. I expect my mate to treat me with respect.* These expectations are not unreasonable, nor do they thwart anyone's self-actualization.

Other expectations reflect a requirement for our mate to *give us* what we need, and they can be unreasonable, as well as thwart our mate's self-actualization. *I need my mate to assure me, everyday, that I am loved. I expect my mate to keep the house clean every day. I expect my mate to make a good living. I expect my mate to spend every evening with me.*

The mate whom we place expectations, also has expectations of us. What are the odds that the all expectations that two people have for each other will be symbiotic? Everyone has needs and they don't always center around what makes one's mate happy. One might have a need to paint a picture rather than clean the house that day. Yet, if this is fulfilled, the mate who expects a clean house every day, might complain.

The reality is that we are all human with some level of insecurity, possessing various qualities, some charming and some afflicted. The question is, will we take responsibility for our own shortcomings upfront, or will we be forced to grow by suffering from constant disappointment that our mate is not making up for what we lack in ourselves: such as confidence, self-worth, or the ability to make peace with one's past?

While it is rewarding to work toward self-actualization, this does not mean that disrespect from a mate should be tolerated. Our mates have an opportunity to understand our sensitive areas. And while it is not the job of our mate to 'save us' neither is it in our best interest to tolerate insensitivity and abuse. Working toward self-actualization is about taking control of our lives and our growth. It is about making healthy decisions regarding what and who is right or wrong for us. If we feel that we are being abused, it is up to us to detach ourselves from that person, and take loving action to better our own lives. Focusing on what we can do to better a situation for ourselves is different than trying to control our mates.

Opposites Attract: *They also repel.*
We are often attracted to those who are strong in areas that we are weak. There is something about someone who can do what we cannot that is most intriguing. Yet, the very quality we might love in another is also the same quality that can come to bother us. The compassionate mates who showers us with love and comfort, might also shower everyone else with love and comfort, leaving us alone more than we'd like. The mates so great at self-defense might also have a wall around their hearts, defending themselves against us.

To help fortify ourselves against the above situations, it is well to work on developing in ourselves what we admire in others, within the scope of our nature. We can also help change our current situation by releasing certain expectations that we have of our mate, and step up to the plate ourselves.

What can you stop expecting in your mate, or in a mate—and develop in yourself to make you feel more secure and capable in your own right? If you are thinking of a future mate replace *my mate*, with *a mate*.

1. *I can stop expecting my mate to_____

and I can start _____.

2. *I can stop expecting my mate to_____

and I can start _____.

3. *I can stop expecting my mate to_____

and I can start _____.

4. *I can stop expecting my mate to_____

and I can start _____.

5. *I can stop expecting my mate to_____

and I can start _____.

We cannot change our partners, but by changing our reactions to our partner's behaviors, we *will* change the relationship. Example: Instead of the typical yelling back when insulted, one can say, *I will not tolerate this*, and instead go for a pleasant walk. A self-respecting act such as this might spark personal growth in our partner. However, if our partner is incapable of personal growth, the relationship might have to end, eventually. If self-actualization is sacrificed, the nature of a troubled relationship will remain, along with painful emotions. This, however, is always and ever—a personal choice.

While it is important to develop ourselves, it is also important to accept our mates or future mates, as they are, whether we continue the relationship or not.

Are there things you expect of your mate that simply go against his or her nature? Example: You expect your mate to be emotionally expressive, but he or she speaks in a succinct monotone manner. Or, you expect your mate to be on time, but he or she hardly ever is. Sometimes, accepting one's mate as is, and focusing on what changes you can make, yields better results. Example: If your mate is always late, have an understanding that you will go ahead with your plans whether he or she is there or not. Example: If your mate is not expressive enough for you, stop trying to beat it out of him or her. Go do something in your life that helps meet your need for more expression, like seeing a play, acting in a play, or starting your own business.

When we release the need for our mate or future mate to be a certain way, and begin to develop ourselves, we are on the path to wholeness. Becoming 'whole' will not only change who we attract in our life, but it will free us to remain or depart from a relationship based upon what is healing for us deep down inside. Self-actualization is reached when we not only grow into our full potential, but when we deem our worth unchangeable by the judgment of anyone. We possess the power to transform our lives, and the meaning of life.

The following exercise is designed to better understand the relationship you have with yourself. Have a conversation with yourself. Speak to yourself as if you are another person, addressing—you.

When I look at you, I . . . Example: *When I look at you, I see a frightened person.*

1. When I look at you, I _____

_____.

2. When I look at you, I _____

_____.

3. When I look at you, I _____

_____.

4. When I look at you, I _____

_____.

5. When I look at you, I _____

_____.

6. When I look at you, I _____

_____.

When I watch you live your life I . . . Example: *When I watch you live your life, I see how you struggle.*

1. When I watch you live your life, I _____

_____.

2. When I watch you live your life, I _____

_____.

3. When I watch you live your life, I _____

_____.

4. When I watch you live your life, I _____

_____.

5. .When I watch you live your life, I _____

_____.

6. When I watch you live your life, I _____

_____.

When I watch you falter, I . . . Example: _When I watch you falter, I feel sorry for you._

1. When I watch you falter, I _____

_____.

2. When I watch you falter, I _____

_____.

3. When I watch you falter, I _____

_____.

4. When I watch you falter, I _____

_____.

5. When I watch you falter, I _____

_____.

6. When I watch you falter, I _____

_____.

When I watch you shine your best, I feel . . . Example: _When I watch you shine your best, I feel proud of you._

1. When I watch you shine your best, I _____

_____.

2. When I watch you shine your best, I _____

_____.

3. When I watch you shine your best, I _____

_____.

4. When I watch you shine your best, I _____

_____.

5. When I watch you shine your best, I _____

_____.

6. When I watch you shine your best, I _____

_____.

Given all this, what compassionate and loving advice can you give yourself?

_____

_____

_____

_____

_____.

What can you do to improve your relationship with yourself?

_____

_____

_____

_____

_____.

If you succeed in these improvements, how do you imagine it might change current or future romantically inclined relationships?

_____

_____

_____.

The more self-actualized you and your current or future mate are, the greater chance there is of having a successful relationship. Become whole in yourself with respect to your nature. Give to yourself what you wish others would give to you in as much as possible. Treat yourself with love, forgiveness, respect, and appreciation. This relationship you have with yourself will become the cornerstone of your relationship with a mate.

Healing and Balancing Exercise for Promoting Positive Relations with Ourselves. We all have healing ability—use it on yourself.

> **Place one hand over your heart.**
> **Place the other hand on top of your head.**
> **Concentrate deeply. Repeat silently or aloud for at least two minutes,**
> **"I appreciate me."**

You have deepened appreciation for yourself, thereby deflecting those who cannot respect you, and attracting those who can.

Relaxation and Creative Visualization Exercise.

Lie in a comfortable position. Play instrumental music that makes you feel good: classical, new age, or music that is gentle, sweeping, or of dynamic beauty. When the music is playing, close your eyes. Inhale through your nose and exhale through your mouth slowly, eight times. Visualize that you are inhaling the power of the universe, which purifies and attunes you physically, emotionally, mentally, and metaphysically. When you exhale, all the tensions and worries leave your body and go back into the universe where they dissolve and blend into the pure life force.

Tighten and loosen your muscles slowly in this order.

Feet. Tighten. Loosen. Take a slow, deep breath, and exhale.
Calves. Tighten. Loosen. Take a slow, deep breath, and exhale.
Thighs. Tighten. Loosen. Take a slow, deep breath, and exhale.
Hips and buttocks. Tighten. Loosen. Take a slow, deep breath, and exhale.
Stomach. Tighten. Loosen. Take a slow, deep breath, and exhale.
Back. Tighten. Loosen. Take a slow, deep breath, and exhale.
Arms. Tighten. Loosen. Take a slow, deep breath, and exhale.
Hands. Tighten. Loosen. Take a slow, deep breath, and exhale.
Neck and shoulders. Tighten. Loosen. Take a slow, deep breath, and exhale.
Face. Tighten. Loosen. Take a slow, deep breath, and exhale.

Then completely relax and take eight more slow, deep breaths. Inhale the universal life energy through your nose and exhale tension through your mouth.

Set the intent: *Whoever I am, whatever I am, whatever I need, whatever is right for me—so be it. I open to insight. I open to receive.*

Now that you are completely relaxed, give yourself over to the music that is playing. Focus inward to your vast self, as vast as the universe. Journey within. You come upon an obscure figure. The figure is *you* not yet formed. Bring definition to the figure by giving it a personality complete with traits and abilities that you desire in the ideal mate.

As the music comes to an end, you know that the more you become your own ideal, the more you will either spark change in your current mate, or attract a mate that will reflect the self-actualization into which you are currently emerging. Rest a few moments, and bask in the experience.

Record your experience.

_____

_____

_____

_____

_____

_____

_____

_____

_____

_____

_____

_____

_____

_____

_____

_____

_____

_____

_____

_____

_____

_____

Draw a picture or symbol that summarizes your experience.

Create a key phrase that summarizes this experience.

_____

When needed, say the mantra silently, and visualize the picture or symbol. This will generate a peaceful, empowered, and clear state of mind.

Δ

Gem of Wisdom
Experiencing life is noble.
There is no failure, no mistake
only innocent exploration with
consequences that drive us
to become more than we are."

Live the Mystery

11

WORKSHOP ELEVEN
HERO, VILLIAN, VICTIM: THE GAMES WE PLAY

True love is a selfless act of *unconditional* compassion toward another. But first, we must give it to ourselves. Only then, can we disengage the shackles that bind us to dysfunctional ways of relating, which center around controlling a mate, or controlling significant others to get them to meet *our* needs, not theirs. When those shackles are gone, the most beautiful relationships can thrive.

For this to happen, it serves to become aware of the dysfunctional games we might play, and some of the primary roles required to play these games. It is almost impossible not to, on occasion, fall into these games, and usually without conscious awareness.

The Dysfunctional Games We Play: Hero, Villain, Victim

The hero, villain, and victim roles in themselves are not dysfunctional. However, they are commonly played in dysfunctional ways.

People who offer a valuable service or help a friend occasionally would not be deemed Dysfunctional Heroes. The dysfunction would be in draining themselves dry to constantly help others, and deriving their worth from saving who they deem 'weaker' people. If so, the Dysfunctional Hero is at play.

Sometimes we have to play the villain to protect ourselves. Other people may not like it if we cause confrontation. The villain role is not dysfunctional unless it is used to demean others in order to boost one's own ego, or to force one's ideas on another by constantly criticizing, thereby conveying to the criticized that they are incompetent. If so, the Dysfunctional Villain is at play.

There are genuine victims in the world, and there are times we have all been victimized in some manner, in some degree. However, if one is constantly in trauma and seems to feed off the trauma, the Dysfunctional Victim is at play.

Sometimes the play is bold. Sometimes it is subtle. Sometimes it only happens for one dramatic scene in our life, or for a bad little period of time. And sometimes—it is chronic.

The Dysfunctional Hero, Villain, and Victim within us (which are interchangeable) lure others around us, into the game. *I will be the victim, you be the hero.* Or, *I will be the villain, you be the victim.* Or, *I will be the hero, you be the villain.* These games are common, seldom identified, and more often rationalized as 'justified' by the players. For this reason, our first response to this exercise may well be, *I don't play those games.* However, it is difficult not to play these games, at least on occasion, because at times we are all insecure. The degree in which these games are played will correlate with the degree of insecurity in the players. Playing these games does not make one bad, only human—deep down, feeling alone and afraid of the dark. However, these tiresome dramas have no end, and yield only temporary comfort.

The Cycle of the Dysfunctional Hero

The Dysfunctional Hero thinks, *Poor you. You need me to help you. People are less competent than I. I must save the world because I am strong, and others are weak.* Dysfunctional Heroes build their worth on neglecting their own needs to save others. The Dysfunctional Hero is compelled to aid the Dysfunctional Victim. This gives the Dysfunctional Hero a sense of importance. However, since the Dysfunctional Victim never stops needing, the Dysfunctional Hero eventually gets frustrated and drained of energy. Thus, the hero becomes the victim. Not comfortable playing that role, the Dysfunctional Hero must create distance with the one being saved, becoming the villain. *After all that I've done for you, you are still messing up. I can't do this anymore.* However, the Dysfunctional Hero, once regenerated and still needing to boost self-worth, will seek out another Dysfunctional Victim, or perhaps the same one. The cycle repeats.

Dysfunctional Heroes are prone to be sacrificial, ignoring their own needs—and constantly and excessively seeking ways to be needed, or people who need them.

The Cycle of the Dysfunctional Victim

Dysfunctional Victims have a poor me attitude. *I am here for others to trample. I always get cheated. People are mean. Life is not fair to me.* Dysfunctional Victims believe deep down that they have fundamental shortcomings, making them unworthy and deserving of punishment. They attract Dysfunctional Villains so that they can be saved by Dysfunctional Heroes, believing they cannot save themselves. When saved, Dysfunctional Victims feel loved and worthy—for a while. To keep the attention of the Dysfunctional Hero, the Dysfunctional Victim must find new and better ways to suffer. Once that is exacted, the Dysfunctional Victim will try to coerce the Dysfunctional Hero to continue saving them. *I can't live without you. I need help. I am weak and you are strong. I need you to save me. Give me love, so I can be all right.* Or, *Give me money, so I can survive.* Or, *Get me out of this mess, or I will die.* If the Dysfunctional Hero tires of saving the Dysfunctional Victim, and shows signs of waning, the Dysfunctional Victim gets mad. *It's your job to save me! You don't care about me! You are just selfish!"* The Dysfunctional Victim has become the villain. Wanting to make amends, the Dysfunctional Victim will become heroic by trying to save the Dysfunctional Hero. *I am sorry. I didn't mean those things I said, and I really think you are great, my hero in fact.* If the Dysfunctional Hero accepts this and assumes the role once again, the cycle repeats. If the Dysfunctional Hero will not accept this and abandons the Dysfunctional Victim, the Dysfunctional Victim will seek a new Dysfunctional Hero, and the cycle goes on.

Dysfunctional Victims are prone to complaining, resisting solutions, chronic illness, and frequent accidents. They chronically invite the criminally minded, or mentally unstable people into their lives.

The Cycle of the Dysfunctional Villain

Dysfunctional Villains blame others instead of taking responsibility for negative life occurrences. Accepting blame would somehow damage their sense of self-worth. Hence, they must deflect blame, assume a critical role, rationalizing that everyone else is deficient compared to them. Dysfunctional Villains believe they were born with a raw deal, and that they have the right to get others to compensate for how they have been cheated. They view others as tools for their personal benefit. Life is about survival. They take advantage of others, so that that no one can take advantage of them. And they take what they need, feeling it's owed them. They thrive by controlling the people around them, which makes them feel powerful, and safe enough to feel that no one can make them the victim. *I am good and great. You must listen to me. My way is always the right way, and you have too many things wrong with you to know how to trust your own judgment.* Eventually Dysfunctional Villains are hated by those they persecute, and thus land the role of victims. Alone and alienated, they will try to entice those they have persecuted, back into game—so that they can play the hero. *You really are competent. You are good and I need you.* Often, the persecuted will gobble these crumbs of approval, and forgive the Dysfunctional Villain. Once the Dysfunctional Villain feels safe, loved, and that control has returned, the cycle repeats. Even if the players change, the cycle repeats.

Dysfunctional Villains are prone to criticize, gossip, and gloat.

How Dysfunctional Victims Break the Game.
Dysfunctional Victims needs to believe in themselves and stand on their own two feet, fight their own battles, and triumph.

How Dysfunctional Villains Break the Game.
Dysfunctional Villains needs to accept their inadequacies, and love themselves anyway, instead of demeaning others to boost their own self-esteem.

How Dysfunctional Heroes Break the Game.
Dysfunctional Heroes need to spend more time tending their own needs, and believe that others have the ability to do the same.

The Healthy Hero
Healthy 'saving' is when the saving does not make you feel drained, angry, scattered, or lost.

Healthy Ways of Dealing with Victimization
Healthy ways of dealing with victimization involve accepting what happened, and exerting personal power to prevent future victimization.

The Healthy Villain
Healthy persecuting involves making self-respecting stands, even if it casts an unwelcome glow. Sometimes you have to be hated to do 'the right thing' for yourself or others.

How This Game Affects You.
How might you have played the game of Dysfunctional Victim, Villain, Hero, at some time in your life? Or how might you be playing it now?

_____

_____

_____

_____

_____

_____

_____

_____

_____

_____

_____.

Explain how the game ended, or explain how it is still in progress.

_____

_____

_____

_____

_____

_____.

If you are in a negative pattern that keeps repeating itself, you are in a dysfunctional game. The game can be broken by believing in yourself, believing in others, taking responsibility for your own happiness, and being true to what feels right for yourself deep down inside.

Healing and Balancing Exercise for Healthy Relating. We all have healing ability—use it on yourself.

> **Place one hand at the base of your breastbone.**
> **Place the other hand over your forehead.**
> **Concentrate deeply. Repeat silently or aloud for at least two minutes.**
> **"Everyone is capable and equal in worth."**

The temptation to fall into a dysfunctional game is now deflected.

Relaxation and Creative Visualization Exercise.

Lie in a comfortable position. Play instrumental music that makes you feel good: classical, new age, or music that is gentle, sweeping, or of dynamic beauty. When the music is playing, close your eyes. Inhale through your nose and exhale through your mouth slowly, eight times. Visualize that you are inhaling the power of the universe, which purifies and attunes you physically, emotionally, mentally, and metaphysically. When you exhale, all the tensions and worries leave your body and go back into the universe where they dissolve and blend into the pure life force.

Tighten and loosen your muscles slowly in this order.

Feet. Tighten. Loosen. Take a slow, deep breath, and exhale.
Calves. Tighten. Loosen. Take a slow, deep breath, and exhale.
Thighs. Tighten. Loosen. Take a slow, deep breath, and exhale.
Hips and buttocks. Tighten. Loosen. Take a slow, deep breath, and exhale.
Stomach. Tighten. Loosen. Take a slow, deep breath, and exhale.
Back. Tighten. Loosen. Take a slow, deep breath, and exhale.
Arms. Tighten. Loosen. Take a slow, deep breath, and exhale.
Hands. Tighten. Loosen. Take a slow, deep breath, and exhale.
Neck and shoulders. Tighten. Loosen. Take a slow, deep breath, and exhale.
Face. Tighten. Loosen. Take a slow, deep breath, and exhale.

Then completely relax and take eight more slow, deep breaths. Inhale the universal life energy through your nose and exhale tension through your mouth.

Set the intent: *Whoever I am, whatever I am, whatever I need, whatever is right for me—so be it. I open to insight. I open to receive.*

Now that you are completely relaxed, give yourself over to the music that is playing. Focus inward to your vast self, as vast as the universe. Journey within. As the music plays, allow yourself to go to the part of you that can play the victim. See the costume. Take it off and behold the needy person beneath (needy for attention). Embrace that part of you with pure love. Then, move to the part of you that can play the villain. See the costume. Take it off and behold the needy person beneath (the need to be right). Embrace that part of you with pure love. Then, move to that part of you that can play the hero. See the costume. Take it off and behold the needy person beneath (needy to be appreciated). Embrace that part of you with pure love.

As the music ends, you feel more secure in your own right. Your selves blend into you, and you have no need to 'play the game.' You feel calm and worthy. Rest a few moments and bask in the experience.

Record your experience.

_____

_____

_____

_____

_____

_____

_____

_____

Draw a picture or symbol that summarizes your experience.

Create a saying that summarizes the experience.

_____

When needed, say the mantra silently, and visualize the picture or symbol. This will generate a peaceful, empowered, and clear state of mind.

Δ

Gem of Wisdom
*The cornerstone
to having healthy relationships
is to have a healthy relationship
with yourself.*

Live the Mystery

12

WORKSHOP TWELVE
YOUR BELIEFS ABOUT YOUSELF

Who are you? This workshop is designed to help you discern *who you are* from *who you are told to be*. We often adopt beliefs about ourselves that came from the outside world (parents, friends, work, school, social groups, mass media, and society as a whole) whether they served us well, or not. Before we can embrace who we really are, we must examine who we have *accepted* we are.

Inside each of us are a myriad of clues, pieces to the puzzle that tell us who we are. We think, feel, dream, imagine, and intuit. Our various bodies are imbued with a variety of traits that distinguish one of us from another. Yet, what is *in us*, and *of us* is most often overlooked for what is outside us (other people, social and physical environment). We compare. We contrast. We look for approval. We often look to the social world to figure out how we must look, how we must act, and what steps we must take to be accepted into the group.

While the social world has its place, it is only the reflection of collective minds. We cannot feed our quintessential being by spoon-feeding an image of ourselves in a mirror. There is no sustenance. Can we learn more about life from watching television, or actually living it? Can we learn more about our quintessential being by giving ourselves to someone else's ideas, or by giving ourselves to our *self*?

So how do we give ourselves to our *self*? How can we come to trust ourselves more than anyone else 'out there?' How do we know who we are apart from the outside world's influence? The answer is simplistic, and yet so often overlooked. To spotlight our individuality, it begins with a simple question. *What healthy action could I take that would be nurturing for me right now, this moment?* The answer might be to take a walk, a bath, express pent up feelings, or maybe *not* to react to something. Sensing what feels healthy and right for us at any given moment, serves as a periscope of sorts to see who we are as unique individuals—and a compass to guide us along our personal path. As we begin to act, think, and feel on our own behalf, we begin to distinguish who we are from how we are *told* to act, think, and feel on the social world's behalf.

Example: The social world might dictate a shower be taken *after* a workout at the gym and not before. But if the answer to the question, *what healthy action could I take that would be nurturing for me right now, this moment?* Is to take a shower *before* going to the gym—then perhaps that shower would take one into a contemplative moment that influences a decision that must be made. Perhaps that urge to take a shower *before* driving to the gym is actually about changing the timing of the drive to avoid an impending accident. We may or may not ever understand the reason, but by *not* betting on ourselves, we are *not* stepping to our own beat. We are *not* feeding our individuality. Even so, we generally do what we think we are supposed to do, over what our senses and intuition indicate is right for us as individuals. We hesitate to trust *ourselves*.

The following exercise is designed to investigate beliefs about yourself that you *may* have adopted from others. The goal is to promote self-understanding, discern what you really believe from what you were led to believe, and to reject the beliefs that do not serve you well.

Beliefs about myself that my mother gave me. (If you had a female guardian instead of mother, replace mom with guardian.) Examples: *My mom led me to believe that I am a drama queen. My mom led me to believe that I am very intelligent.*

My mom led me to believe _____.

My mom led me to believe _____.

My mom led me to believe _____.

My mom led me to believe _____.

My mom led me to believe _____.

But . . . who are you—really?

Now, restate each answer above, and add on, *but the truth about me is . . .* If you were not assessed correctly, explain. Example: *The truth about me is that I am not a drama queen—I just feel things deeply. I am very sensitive.* If you were assessed somewhat correctly but it is not the complete picture, explain. Example: *The truth about me is that while I am a drama queen, the feelings are real.* If you were assessed correctly, give more information. Example: *The truth about me is that I am a drama queen. I love attention. I think it is because my dad left our family when I was young.*

1. *My mom led me to believe_____,

but the truth about me is_____

_____.

2. *My mom led me to believe _____,

but the truth about me is_____

_____.

3. *My mom led me to believe_____,

but the truth about me is_____

_____.

4. *My mom led me to believe _____,

but the truth about me is_____

_____.

Beliefs about myself that my father gave me. (If you had a male guardian instead of a dad, replace dad with guardian.) Example: *My dad led me to believe that I am special because I get good grades. My dad led me to believe that I am worthless because I act out.*

1. My dad led me to believe _____.

2. My dad led me to believe _____.

3. My dad led me to believe _____.

4. My dad led me to believe _____.

5. My dad led me to believe _____.

But . . . who are you—really?

Now, restate each answer above and add on, *but the truth about me is . . .* If you were not assessed correctly, explain. Example: *The truth about me is that I am not special for getting good grades. I didn't get good grades. I cheated, but I cheated because he put so much pressure on me to get good grades.* If you were assessed somewhat correctly but it is not the complete picture, explain. Example: *The truth about me is that I am special but not because I got straight A's in school. It is because I am an innovative thinker, and I have the courage to act upon my innovation.* If you were assessed correctly, give more information. Example: *The truth about me is that I was a special kid. I got good grades, and all my friends came to me for help.*

1. *My dad led me to believe _____,

but the truth about me is _____

_____.

2. *My dad led me to believe_____,

but the truth about me is _____

_____.

3. *My dad led me to believe _____,

but the truth about me is _____

_____.

4. *My dad led me to believe _____,

but the truth about me is _____

_____.

5. *My dad led me to believe _____,

but the truth about me is _____

_____.

Beliefs about myself that my friends gave me. Different friends may have led you to believe different things or the same things. Even if they differ, fill in the blanks. Examples: *My friends led me to believe that I am an oddball. My friends led me to believe that I am funny.*

1. My friends led me to believe _____.

2. My friends led me to believe _____.

3. My friends led me to believe _____.

4. My friends led me to believe _____.

5. My friends led me to believe _____.

But . . . who are you—really?

Now, restate each answer above and add on, *but the truth about me is . . .* If you were not assessed correctly, explain. Example: *The truth about me is that I was not an oddball—I just had friends who were not compatible with me.* If you were assessed somewhat correctly but it is not the complete picture, explain. Example: *The truth about me is that what they call oddball—is really just me being myself, instead of faking who I am just to fit in.* If you were assessed correctly, give more information. Example: *The truth about me is that I am odd-ball, and proud of it.*

1. *My friends led me to believe _____,

but the truth about me is_____

_____.

2. *My friends led me to believe _____,

but the truth about me is_____

_____.

3. *My friends led me to believe _____,

but the truth about me is_____

_____.

4. *My friends led me to believe _____,

but the truth about me is_____

_____.

5. *My friends led me to believe _____,

but the truth about me is_____

_____.

Beliefs about myself that my job world gave me. Different job experiences may have led you to believe different things or the same things. Even if they differ, fill in the blanks. Examples: *My job world led me to believe that I am a good manager. My job world led me to believe that I stink at public relations.*

1. My job world led me to believe _____.

2. My job world led me to believe _____.

3. My job world led me to believe _____.

4. My job world led me to believe _____.

5. My job world led me to believe _____.

But . . . who are you—really?

Now, restate each answer above and add on, *but the truth about me is . . .* If you were not assessed correctly, explain. Example: *The truth about me is that I am not really that good of a manager. I just seem to be better than previous managers.* If you were assessed somewhat correctly, but it is not the complete picture, explain. Example: *The truth about me is that I am a good manager, but only in the restaurant business.* If you were assessed correctly, give more information. Example: *The truth about me is that though I am a great manager, it takes a lot out of me, and sometimes I am too tired to socialize later.*

1. *My job world led me to believe _____,

but the truth about me is_____

_____.

2. *My job world led me to believe _____,

but the truth about me is_____

_____.

3. *My job world led me to believe _____,

but the truth about me is_____

_____.

4. *My job world led me to believe _____,

but the truth about me is_____

_____.

5. *My job world led me to believe _____,

but the truth about me is_____

_____.

Beliefs about myself that the mass media gave me. Examples: _The mass media led me to believe that I am lacking because I don't appear like a model. The mass media led me to believe that it is okay not to cringe every time that I see violence on television, video games, or the big screen._

1. The mass media led me to believe_____.

2. The mass media led me to believe_____.

3. The mass media led me to believe_____.

4. The mass media led me to believe_____.

5. The mass media led me to believe_____.

Who are you—really?

Now, restate each answer above and add on, _but the truth about me is . . ._ If the belief does not fit who you really are, explain. Example: _The truth about me is that I do not feel like I am lacking because I don't look like a model, because my self-esteem is very high._ If the belief somewhat fits, but it is not the complete picture, explain. Example: _The truth about me is that my self-esteem does waver because I don't look like a model, but I am trying to counter_ *that.* If the belief fits, give more information. Example: *I do feel like I am lacking because I don't look like a model.*

1. *The mass media led me to believe_____,

but the truth about me is _____

_____.

2. *The mass media led me to believe_____,

but the truth about me is _____

_____.

3. *The mass media led me to believe_____,

but the truth about me is _____

_____.

4. *The mass media led me to believe_____,

but the truth about me is _____

_____.

5. *The mass media led me to believe_____,

but the truth about me is _____

_____.

Beliefs about myself that society (the social world as a whole) led me to believe:
This can be tied in with the mass media—however, it exceeds what the mass media generates.
Examples: *Society led me to believe that I am worth the amount of money that I make. Society led me to believe that appearance is more important than what is in my heart.*

1. Society led me to believe _____.

2. Society led me to believe _____.

3. Society led me to believe _____.

4. Society led me to believe _____.

5. Society led me to believe _____.

But . . . who are you—really?

Now, restate each answer above and add on, *but the truth about me is . . .* If the belief does not fit who you really are, explain. Example: *The truth about me is that even though I don't make a lot of money, I deem myself valuable, because to me being a good person is more important than my financial status.* If the belief somewhat fits you, but it is not the complete picture, explain. Example: *The truth about me is that even though I know I am worth more than my financial status, I still feel unimportant for having a low income, but I don't really think that I am unimportant.* If the belief does fit you, give more information. *The truth about me is that I do feel financial status measures worth because I worked my way up from poverty to make a good living, and that says something for my abilities.*

1. *Society led me to believe _____,

but the truth about me is_____

_____.

2. *Society led me to believe _____,

but the truth about me is_____

_____.

3. *Society led me to believe _____,

but the truth about me is_____

_____.

4. *Society led me to believe _____,

but the truth about me is_____

_____.

5. *Society led me to believe _____,

but the truth about me is_____

_____

6. *Society led me to believe _____,

but the truth about me is_____

_____.

You may have discovered that you have adopted beliefs that you would rather discard. If so, list them below.

1. I refuse to believe that _____.

2. I refuse to believe that _____.

3. I refuse to believe that _____.

4. I refuse to believe that _____.

5. I refuse to believe that _____.

6. I refuse to believe that _____.

7. I refuse to believe that _____.

Now that you have clarified who you are, or at least who you want to be, *apart from outside influence*, bring that part of you to the forefront of your being. Let it shine.

Healing and Balancing Exercise for Being Who You Truly Are. We all have healing ability—use it on yourself.

> **Place one hand at the base of your breastbone.**
> **Place the other hand on top of your head.**
> **Concentrate deeply. Repeat silently or aloud for at least five minutes,**
> **"I give myself to myself."**

Your allegiance is strengthened to be true to yourself, not the ideas of the others.

Relaxation and Creative Visualization Exercise.

Lie in a comfortable position. Play instrumental music that makes you feel good: classical, new age, or music that is gentle, sweeping, or of dynamic beauty. When the music is playing, close your eyes. Inhale through your nose, and exhale through your mouth slowly, eight times. Visualize that you are inhaling the power of the universe, which purifies and attunes you physically, emotionally, mentally, and metaphysically. When you exhale, all the tensions and worries leave your body and go back into the universe where they dissolve and blend into the pure life force.

Tighten and loosen your muscles slowly in this order.

Feet. Tighten. Loosen. Take a slow, deep breath, and exhale.
Calves. Tighten. Loosen. Take a slow, deep breath, and exhale.
Thighs. Tighten. Loosen. Take a slow, deep breath, and exhale.
Hips and buttocks. Tighten. Loosen. Take a slow, deep breath, and exhale.
Stomach. Tighten. Loosen. Take a slow, deep breath, and exhale.
Back. Tighten. Loosen. Take a slow, deep breath, and exhale.
Arms. Tighten. Loosen. Take a slow, deep breath, and exhale.
Hands. Tighten. Loosen. Take a slow, deep breath, and exhale.
Neck and shoulders. Tighten. Loosen. Take a slow, deep breath, and exhale.

Face. Tighten. Loosen. Take a slow, deep breath, and exhale.

Then completely relax and take eight more slow, deep breaths. Inhale the universal life energy through your nose and exhale tension through your mouth.

Set the intent: *Whoever I am, whatever I am, whatever I need, whatever is right for me—so be it. I open to insight. I open to receive.*

Now that you are completely relaxed, give yourself over to the music that is playing. Focus inward to your vast self, as vast as the universe. Journey within. Imagine that you a very large bird flying in the sky, but you are encumbered with mud clumps that make it hard to fly. The clumps are beliefs that you have adopted that are not in your own best interest. Every time you flap your wings to shake off the mud, think of a belief that you want to release. You can keep flying as you do this, or land somewhere, and flap your wings. Keep focusing on beliefs you want to shed because they weigh you down. As the mud is shaken from you, so are these beliefs that hurt you. When the mud is off, a gentle rain comes down, and washes you clean. Then you take to the sky, free to be you. Rejuvenate.

When the music ends, you feel empowered to emanate your true self. Rest a few moments and bask in the experience.

Record your experience.

_____

_____

_____

_____

_____

_____

_____

_____

_____

_____

_____

_____

Draw a picture or symbol that summarizes your experience.

Create a key phrase that summarizes this experience.

_____

When needed, say the mantra silently, and visualize the picture or symbol. This will generate a peaceful, empowered, and clear state of mind.

$$\Delta$$

Gem of Wisdom
In the kaleidoscope of the many parts and people
moving around us, it is easy to get confused.
So, close your eyes and listen to that tiny voice deep within
that knows what is truly healthy for you.
Heed that voice, above all others.

Live the Mystery

13

WORKSHOP THIRTEEN
YOUR BELIEFS ABOUT THE WORLD

People, in general, search for something to believe in. If we can be intellectually convinced or emotionally persuaded, almost anything can become what one 'believes' in. *I believe money is the key to happiness. I believe in people. I believe our government is corrupt. I believe in fate. I believe it is a dog eat dog world. I believe there is much beauty in the world.* These beliefs cement us into a certain kind of reality. Seldom do our beliefs stem from seeing the whole picture, but rather a portion of the picture. Therefore, believing only this or that can limit us profoundly from discovering not only all that the world has to offer, but also the rest of who we are. This is not to suggest that one abandon the beliefs one has—but more pointedly, to *expand* the beliefs one has. In a sense, it is opening to the bounty of life.

At times, we don't know what to believe or who to believe, and we turn everywhere but where we can go to end the search—to a state of mind that is far more rewarding than any discovery 'out there.' This state of mind involves loosening one's self from being relegated to any particular way of thinking. What is—is, despite our beliefs. Opening to *what is* beyond what we know, can yield the most wonderful experiences. And, opening to the idea that there is more to the world and to each one of us than we can fathom, invites amazing discoveries.

This next exercise is designed to help you examine your beliefs and perhaps loosen the cement that keeps them in place, the cement that keeps you confined to a smaller way of life than what is possible.

What are your general beliefs about romantic love? Feel free to rant, or lecture.
Examples: *My general beliefs about romantic love are that romantic love is a sham for the most part, or if it isn't, true love is almost non-existent. I don't think . . .*

My general beliefs about romantic love are _____

_____

_____

_____

_____

_____.

So, that is what I think about romantic love (leave blank for now) _____

In what way have these beliefs about romantic love affected your daily life? Example: *I feel defensive when someone wants a romantic relationship with me. I don't try to find a partner anymore . . .*

_____

_____

_____.

Some beliefs bring us peace of mind and make our lives better. Other beliefs cause conflict and tension. Either way, your beliefs about romantic love are kept in place by your perception. Our perceptions only reflect *some* truth. Life is so vast, it is unlikely that anyone's perceptions could reflect the *whole* truth. Without discounting your perception, you can allow yourself the opportunity to expand your perception, by adding the word MAYBE.

Example: *So, that is what I think about romantic love*—MAYBE.

If you choose to open, go back to the end of the paragraph that describes your beliefs about romantic love and insert the word, MAYBE.

What are your general beliefs about love? Feel free to rant or lecture. Example: *Regarding love in the world, I think people are forgetting about love and trying too hard to make money, stay in control, and fit images. I think . . .*

My general beliefs about love are _____

_____

_____

_____

_____

_____.

So, that is what I believe about love (leave blank for now) _____

In what way have these beliefs about love affected your daily life? Example: *I feel like love is diminishing, so I try to be more loving everywhere I go. I practice random acts of kindness. I try to put a smile on people's faces . . .*

_____

_____

_____.

Without discounting your perception, you can allow yourself the opportunity to expand your perception by adding the word MAYBE. By doing this, you open yourself up to any truths you may have not yet discovered.

Example: *So, that is what I think about love in general—MAYBE.*

If you choose to open, go back to the end of the paragraph that describes your beliefs about love and insert the word, MAYBE.

What are your general beliefs about people? Feel free to rant or lecture. Example: *I think people are doing the best they can even though the news gives people a bad impression. I think . . .*

My general beliefs about people are _____

_____

_____

_____

_____

_____

_____.

So, that is what I believe about people (leave blank for now) _____

In what way have these beliefs about people affected your daily life? Example: *I give people a lot of chances because I think deep down they are good. I give to a lot of charities. I try not to judge . . .*

_____

_____

_____.

Without discounting your perception, you can allow yourself the opportunity to expand your perception by adding the word MAYBE. By doing this, you open yourself up to any truths you may have not yet discovered.
Example: *So, that is what I think about people—MAYBE.*
If you choose to open, go back to the end of the paragraph that describes your beliefs about people and insert the word, MAYBE.

What are your general beliefs about the world? Feel free to rant or lecture. Example: *I think the world is going to pot and it is too late to save it, and . . .*

My general beliefs about the world are _____

_____

_____

_____

_____

_____

_____ .

So, that is what I believe about the world (leave blank for now) _____

In what way have these beliefs about the world affected your daily life? Example: *I have three locks on every door, and an alarm system, and . . .*

_____

_____

_____ .

Without discounting your perception, you can allow yourself the opportunity to *expand* your perception by adding the word MAYBE. By doing this, you open yourself up to any truths you may have not yet discovered.

Example: *So, that is what I think about the world—MAYBE.*

If you choose to open, go back to the end of the paragraph that describes your beliefs about the world and insert the word, MAYBE.

What are your general beliefs about life? Feel free to rant or lecture. Example: *I think life is a great gift because even though it is challenging . . .*

My general beliefs about life are _____

_____

_____

_____

_____

_____.

So, that is what I believe about life (leave blank for now) _____

In what way have these beliefs affected your daily life? Example: *I have an attitude of appreciation. I adventure out into the world . . . .*

_____

_____

_____.

Without discounting your perception, you can allow yourself the opportunity to *expand* your perception by adding the word MAYBE. By doing this, you open yourself up to any truths you may have not yet discovered.

Example: *So, that is what I think about life—MAYBE.*

If you choose to open, go back to the end of the paragraph that describes your beliefs about life and insert the word, MAYBE.

Whatever our beliefs, if we open our minds to the idea that there is more to the picture than what we believe, more to the people around us than what we know, and more to ourselves than we can fathom—then we invite the possibility of flying into the overview to experience the panoramic life picture, and all the colors of the rainbow instead of being locked in one scene, one color, one way, for our whole life. There is *always* a larger picture, and *always* more to understand, and *always* deeper realms of illumination and joy to experience. Remaining open, gives us the freedom and opportunity to enrich our lives.

Healing and Balancing Exercise for Opening. We all have healing ability—use it on yourself.

> **Place one hand beneath your navel.**
> **Place the other hand on top of your head.**
> **Concentrate deeply. Repeat silently or aloud for at least two minutes,**
> **"I open to the wonder of life."**

Now the cement that keeps you locked into a limited reality is loosened.

Relaxation and Creative Visualization Exercise.
Lie down in a comfortable position. Play instrumental music that makes you feel good: classical, new age, or music that is gentle, sweeping, or of dynamic beauty. When the music is playing, close your eyes. Inhale through your nose, and exhale through your mouth slowly, eight times. Visualize that you are inhaling the power of the universe, which purifies and at tunes you physically, emotionally, mentally, and metaphysically. When you exhale, all the tensions and worries leave your body and go back into the universe where they dissolve and blend into the pure life force.

Tighten and loosen your muscles slowly in this order.

Feet. Tighten. Loosen. Take a slow, deep breath, and exhale.
Calves. Tighten. Loosen. Take a slow, deep breath, and exhale.
Thighs. Tighten. Loosen. Take a slow, deep breath, and exhale.
Hips and buttocks. Tighten. Loosen. Take a slow, deep breath, and exhale.
Stomach. Tighten. Loosen. Take a slow, deep breath, and exhale.
Back. Tighten. Loosen. Take a slow, deep breath, and exhale.
Arms. Tighten. Loosen. Take a slow, deep breath, and exhale.
Hands. Tighten. Loosen. Take a slow, deep breath, and exhale.
Neck and shoulders. Tighten. Loosen. Take a slow, deep breath, and exhale.
Face. Tighten. Loosen. Take a slow, deep breath, and exhale.

Then completely relax and take eight more slow, deep breaths. Inhale the universal life energy through your nose and exhale tension through your mouth.

Set the intent: *Whoever I am, whatever I am, whatever I need, whatever is right for me—so be it. I open to insight. I open to receive.*

Now that you are completely relaxed, give yourself over to the music that is playing. Focus inward to your vast self, as vast as the universe. Journey within and move deeper inside yourself than you have ever before. As the human that you are, imagine that you can fly. You are flying into the whole majesty of life, whatever it is. You are safe and empowered because your intent to open, and flower into your full potential, is pure. Leave your binocular viewpoints behind. Allow your current perceptions of reality to broaden so that singular beliefs won't blind you to the panoramic view. Experience the beauty of all you are, beyond what you comprehend. Experience this free flight, sometimes moving into layers of color, or scenes of beauty. Then you move higher and higher until you are out in the universe, and you can see the earth below you. Such wonder! You can sense that there is more to life than perhaps you can ever know. Allow yourself to remain open to infinite wisdom, like a tree that never stops becoming more beautiful, for it will not say no to a new leaf sprouting. Now, you descend, slowly, back to the earth, until you feel yourself laying comfortably, listening to music.

When the music ends, you will feel open to the whole picture of life beyond what you intellectually know. Colors will seem richer. Life will seem brighter. And you will feel expanded. Rest a few moments and bask in the experience.

Record your experience.

_____

_____

_____

_____

_____

_____

_____

_____

_____

_____

Draw a picture or symbol that summarizes your experience.

Create a key phrase that summarizes this experience.

_____

When needed, say the mantra silently, and visualize the picture or symbol. This will generate a peaceful, empowered, and clear state of mind.

Δ

Gem of Wisdom
Those who see the larger picture,
can better appreciate
the binocular view.

Live the Mystery

14

WORKSHOP FOURTEEN
HIGHWAY TO THE STARS-KEEPING FOCUS

The world can seem a chaotic place with multiple scenes playing all at once. These diversions often gain our attention, and the next thing we know we have lost our sense of life direction, or we have put it on hold. Either way, we are off course from our path in life, and maybe even on someone else's. There is a sense of loss, a scattered feeling, accompanied with depression or anger.

When we are on our path, there is a sense of empowerment and contentment, and an enthusiastic charge that fills the body, mind, and heart. It is like we are on a highway to the stars, into the mystery and beauty of existence.

Remaining on that path throughout our lives is key to getting to where we are going, which is our own self-actualization, the personal transformation into the full fruition of who we truly are, and the life we are meant to live. Staying on course requires that we detach our sense of worth from other people's reactions to us. And it requires that we embrace our worth—on its own merit, not anyone else's.

Sometimes we feel that if we truly take care of ourselves that others around us might suffer. We don't have to sacrifice our own path to keep someone else on theirs. On the deepest levels, everyone is a giant and can find their own way 'home,' with or without us. To think otherwise is a slam to every human being, a belief that they are less than us. This is not to say that we all don't play a significant part in each other's lives. We do. This is not to say, don't lend a helping hand. We must. However, all too often, we are more caught up in the lives of others rather than paying attention to how we can improve our own. If we do, or do not, based on what makes us feel bright, clear, and enthusiastic, then we can stay on course, and still be loving toward others.

The difficulty arises when those around us don't like the path we are on, and they react in an effort to get us on the path that *they* want us on. In this, we must be committed to follow our highway to the stars—no matter what caterwauling, threats, demands, peacock strutting, or pleading, is going on around us. Yes, sometimes the people around us will be upset when we take care of ourselves, because suddenly they are forced to take more responsibility for their own lives and their own happiness.

The greatest example we can be to anyone is to follow our own path with dedication and dignity. In that, we unleash the shine and glimmer of our quintessence—a living example that 'enlightenment' doesn't require money, image, age, or trophies for the mantel. In the chaotic midst of people running around banging into each other, influenced by the mass media, social groups, and significant others—we will be walking the highway to the stars with streaks of flaming light stretching far behind us. For we see, and we hear, and we feel the pulse of life in its pure and natural state. In that, we find comfort, and inspiration. In that, we find ourselves in our greatest and most magnificent form.

Taking steps along our path requires satisfying yearnings that stem from a need to *nurture ourselves on the deepest levels.* These yearnings are things we can satisfy that *do not* require anyone else *sacrificing or being sacrificed.* Examples: having an affair, leaving children unattended to go have fun, coercing another to do something with us. These yearnings are not about following one's path, but about covering up pain, and using or abusing others to do it.

Meeting deep down yearnings in a healthy manner that nurtures and heals us deep within, is about taking steps that are in keeping with who are as a unique human being. These are pure acts, from our hearts, and they make us shine. Examples: oil painting, jogging, reading to a child, having a baby, watching a sunset, hiking, a good conversation, petting a kitten, cooking, dancing, meditating, decorating one's house or body, putting together a business deal, performing on stage, diagnosing illness, playing sports, making clothes, doing woodwork, tending a garden, feeding the birds, volunteering somewhere. Even if the yearnings cannot be met in one way, such as not being able to produce children when a baby is wanted badly, there are *always* ways to nurture self and to feel whole inside. All that's needed is a little creativity, patience, and faith in yourself and your life path.

The following exercise is designed to help you pinpoint what steps you could take to stay focused on your 'Highway to the Stars.'

What do you yearn for that would *nourish you on the deepest levels,* that *does not* result in others sacrificing or being sacrificed?

1. I yearn _____.

2. I yearn _____.

3. I yearn _____.

4. I yearn _____.

5. I yearn _____.

6. I yearn _____.

7. I yearn _____.

8. I yearn _____.

9. I yearn _____.

10. I yearn _____.

List common obstacles rooted in yourself that keep you from walking your path. Examples: *An obstacle to walking my path is that I fear what people might think of me. On obstacle to walking my path is that I fear something bad might happen to me. An obstacle to walking my path is that I doubt my abilities. An obstacle to walking my path is that I have a bad temper and I get distracted with the drama's I create. An obstacle to walking my path is that I feel guilty and undeserving of happiness.*

1. *An obstacle to walking my path is_____

_____.

2. *An obstacle to walking my path is_____

_____.

3. *An obstacle to walking my path is_____

_____.

4. *An obstacle to walking my path is_____

_____.

5. *An obstacle to walking my path is_____

_____.

These obstacles likely highlight doubts and fears, feelings of being incapable, or unworthy. What must you do to remove these obstacles? Example: *To get past my guilt, I must forgive myself. To get past what others might think of me, I must love myself enough to not to care.*

1. *To get past _____

I must _____.

2. *To get past _____

I must _____.

3. *To get past _____

I must _____.

4. *To get past _____

I must _____.

5. *To get past _____

I must _____.

Focus now on your strengths, on what makes you uniquely *you*. What strengths do you possess to help you get past the obstacles that keep you from walking your path? Examples: tenacity, open-mindedness, conviction, joy for life, assertiveness, meditative, independent, faith, bravery, sensitivity, philosophical nature.

To walk my path, I will use the following strengths that I possess:

_____

_____

_____

Healing and Balancing Exercise for Staying Focused. We all have healing ability—use it on yourself.

> **Place one hand at the base of your breastbone.**
> **Place the other hand over your heart.**
> **Concentrate deeply. Repeat silently or aloud for at least two minutes.**
> **"I believe in my story."**

You now can be true to your own story and not be deflected to give it up for the story of another.

Relaxation and Creative Visualization Exercise.

Lie in a comfortable position. Play instrumental music that makes you feel good: classical, new age, or music that is gentle, sweeping, or of dynamic beauty. When the music is playing, close your eyes. Inhale through your nose and exhale through your mouth slowly, eight times. Visualize that you are inhaling the power of the universe, which purifies and attunes you physically, emotionally, mentally, and metaphysically. When you exhale, all the tensions and worries leave your body and go back into the universe where they dissolve and blend into the pure life force.

Tighten and loosen your muscles slowly in this order.

Feet. Tighten. Loosen. Take a slow, deep breath, and exhale.
Calves. Tighten. Loosen. Take a slow, deep breath, and exhale.
Thighs. Tighten. Loosen. Take a slow, deep breath, and exhale.
Hips and buttocks. Tighten. Loosen. Take a slow, deep breath, and exhale.
Stomach. Tighten. Loosen. Take a slow, deep breath, and exhale.
Back. Tighten. Loosen. Take a slow, deep breath, and exhale.
Arms. Tighten. Loosen. Take a slow, deep breath, and exhale.
Hands. Tighten. Loosen. Take a slow, deep breath, and exhale.
Neck and shoulders. Tighten. Loosen. Take a slow, deep breath, and exhale.
Face. Tighten. Loosen. Take a slow, deep breath, and exhale.

Then completely relax and take eight more, slow, deep breaths. Inhale the universal life energy through your nose, exhale tension through your mouth.

Set the intent: *Whoever I am, whatever I am, whatever I need, whatever is right for me—so be it. I open to insight. I open to receive.*

Now that you are completely relaxed, give yourself over to the music that is playing. Focus inward to your vast self, as vast as the universe. Journey within. See yourself moving along your path in life. Take notice of who or what is on the sidelines, saying or doing what can pull you off course. You move forth on your path without being distracted. Ahead, you see a being of light. This being is *you* in full fruition, wise and glowing. Move toward that being with a conviction in your heart—and don't look back.

As the music ends, embrace your determination to stay focused on *your* path. Rest a few moments and bask in the experience.

Record your experience.

_____

_____

_____

_____

_____

_____

_____

_____

_____

_____

_____

_____

_____

_____

Draw your path. Draw what is on the path or the sides of the path that distract you and sometimes derail you. Draw what is at end of the path.

Create a key phrase that you can say to yourself to help you keep focus on 'your highway to the stars.'

_____

When needed, say the mantra silently, and visualize the picture or symbol. This will generate a peaceful, empowered, and clear state of mind.

Δ

Gem of Wisdom
The actualizing of a thousand dreams
rests on one thing—
Sinking into your true and natural self.
The rest will come.

Live the Mystery

15

WORKSHOP FIFTEEN
CENTEREDNESS: INTERNAL STENGTH

The Highway to the Stars is our personal path. However, remaining on our personal path is made much easier when we practice centering. Centering gives us a strong, clear presence within ourselves.

It is easy to be swept into the current of our environment, be it a trip to the store, our place of employment, or family members. To hold one's own in the face of others can be a daunting task indeed. As humans, we yearn to belong. To belong, we will usually do almost anything, even if the price we pay is sacrificing belief in ourselves. We might be enthusiastic about an idea, but those around us call it stupid. To exact the idea anyway is the great challenge.

We might see something from an angle no one else can, yet the force of another's opinion is so strong, we might doubt ourselves. We might have our own sense of things, yet surrender to charismatic people's way of thinking. We might feel great about ourselves one moment, and then someone treats us bad and we feel sad or mad the next. Oh, how easily we can be knocked down!

Centeredness is about holding on to who we are, *no matter what*! Though it is favorable to remove ourselves from environments and people who are psychologically toxic to us, if we cannot, we can still remain centered, and *not* react.

Centeredness comes from a place deep inside the core of our being. It is the wellspring of our essence. When we are in it, we feel strong and bright and clear in our own right. From there we move differently, act differently, see and feel differently. We change our experience of reality from hazy, confused, lost, alone, and angry—to an arrow flying toward the bulls-eye, the river flowing toward the mighty sea, the atom beholding itself as the universe—small and large at the same time.

Beneath the surface wrapping and conscious acceptance of who we are, based on outside influence, is our true self. Our true self is vast, wise, and potent. It is in tune with the power of the cosmic whole—the ocean, the earth, the universe. It is in tune with the power that moves the stars, circulates blood, and turns the seasons. When we move inward into that power, we behold our uniqueness, and our sameness. We understand our nature, and sense our place in life. We find ease in being true to who we are beyond conscious analysis. Imagine a butterfly trying to act like a grasshopper, or a tree trying to be a flower, or a grain of sand that always envies the seashell, instead of beholding the grandeur of its own unique nature. Perhaps that jealous grain of sand just doesn't know how many poems have been written about it, or how beautiful it sparkles in the sun, or how a child's hand scoops it up feeling delight as it slips through fingers back to the ground. Being one's self is vital to the process of 'becoming,' and to experiencing bliss.

When we are centered, we feel bright and brave, no matter what is going on around us. We feel at our best. State those times below. Examples: *I feel centered when I am singing. I feel centered when I am nurturing my children.*

1. I feel centered when _____.

2. I feel centered when _____.

3. I feel centered when _____.

4. I feel centered when _____.

5. I feel centered when _____.

6. I feel centered when _____.

7. I feel centered when _____.

8. I feel centered when _____.

9. I feel centered when _____.

10. I feel centered when _____.

When we are not centered, or off center—we often feel low, scattered, vulnerable, and reactive to even small things. State these times below. Examples: *I feel off center when I am alone too long. I feel off-center when I get rejected.*

1. I feel off-center when _____.

2. I feel off-center when _____.

3. I feel off-center when _____.

4. I feel off-center when _____.

5. I feel off-center when _____.

6. I feel off-center when _____.

7. I feel off-center when _____.

8. I feel off-center when _____.

9. I feel off-center when _____.

10. I feel off-center when _____.

Though certain activities might make us feel centered, and others make us feel weak—centeredness is ultimately a state of mind, and can be experienced no matter what one is doing or what one has done. It is a place *within* us where all worries are released, and a calm healing power resides. Practice and use the following centering exercise whenever needed. It will quell nervousness, fear, guilt, anger, pain, and confusion. It will create a sense of calm, clarity, security, and empowerment.

Healing and Balancing Exercise for Centering. We all have healing ability—use it on yourself. This exercise works well under the night sky, but is effective anywhere.

Hold one palm of your hand to the universe, and the other palm to the earth. Imagine the energy of the universe coming into the hand open to the sky, flowing through your body, and going out the hand that is open to the earth. Repeat silently or aloud for at least two minutes, "The Creative Life Force is moving through me—I feel it now."

A calming, yet empowering energy now centers you beyond the reach of outside influence.

Relaxation and Creative Visualization Exercise.

Lie in a comfortable position. Play instrumental music that makes you feel good: classical, new age, or music that is gentle, sweeping, or of dynamic beauty. When the music is playing, close your eyes. Inhale through your nose, and exhale through your mouth slowly, eight times. Visualize that you are inhaling the power of the universe, which purifies and attunes you physically, emotionally, mentally, and metaphysically. When you exhale, all the tensions and worries leave your body and go back into the universe where they dissolve and blend into the pure life force.

Tighten and loosen your muscles slowly in this order.

Feet. Tighten. Loosen. Take a slow, deep breath, and exhale.
Calves. Tighten. Loosen. Take a slow, deep breath, and exhale.
Thighs. Tighten. Loosen. Take a slow, deep breath, and exhale.
Hips and buttocks. Tighten. Loosen. Take a slow, deep breath, and exhale.
Stomach. Tighten. Loosen. Take a slow, deep breath, and exhale.
Back. Tighten. Loosen. Take a slow, deep breath, and exhale.
Arms. Tighten. Loosen. Take a slow, deep breath, and exhale.
Hands. Tighten. Loosen. Take a slow, deep breath, and exhale.
Neck and shoulders. Tighten. Loosen. Take a slow, deep breath, and exhale.
Face. Tighten. Loosen. Take a slow, deep breath, and exhale.

Then completely relax and take eight more slow, deep breaths. Inhale the universal life energy through your nose and exhale tension through your mouth.

Set the intent: *Whoever I am, whatever I am, whatever I need, whatever is right for me—so be it. I open to insight. I open to receive.*

Now that you are completely relaxed, give yourself over to the music that is playing. Focus inward to your vast self, as vast as the universe. Journey within to the core of your being which is the center point of who you are beyond what you understand. Concentrate on remaining still at this centered point, like being at the center of a wheel or in the eye of a tornado, while all else around you spins in motion. Keep your vision turned inward. You might feel your head buzzing, or a sensation of inward motion. Keep your focus, not allowing other thoughts or feelings to interfere. Just . . . listen. Just . . . experience. You will begin to feel great strength and clarity. If an epiphany emerges, you will remember it. This is the place of clearing out all the commotion and chatter from everywhere by remaining very still, in the center of everything.

As the music ends, you will carry this centeredness with you into your daily life. Rest a few minutes and bask in the experience.

Record your experience.

_____

_____

_____

_____

_____

_____

_____

_____

_____

_____

_____

_____

_____

_____

Draw a picture or symbol that summarizes your experience.

Create a key phrase that summarizes the experience.

_____

When needed, say the mantra silently, and visualize the picture or symbol. This will generate a peaceful, empowered, and clear state of mind.

Δ

Gem of Wisdom
You find peace in the outer world
by finding peace in the inner world.

Live the Mystery

Date_____

16

CHAPTER SIXTEEN
MULTI-LEVEL AWARENESS: YOU IN NATURE

Often, we are so involved with our own reality, and the realities of those around us, that we are blind and deaf to the bigger picture that reveals so much beauty. Sometimes if we allow ourselves to expand our mind and life experience into that beauty, we find in some way, a great connection to it. In that connection, we do not feel so locked into our bodies, like an island unto itself, separated from everything else. Instead, we can begin to breathe in the natural wonders of our planet in all its splendor. We can begin to see the synchronicity in natural law, and in ourselves. Our small world becomes larger in the most beautiful way.

The following exercises are designed to bring you closer to the healing powers in our living planet.

Earth. Wind. Water. Fire. Which *currently* attracts you most? _____

What about this element, attracts you? Example: *This element quells my anxiety and makes me feel clean and free.*

_____

_____.

What color *currently* attracts you the most? _____

What feelings does this color evoke? Example: *This color makes me feel calm like I don't have a care in the world.*

_____

_____.

What season currently attracts you the most? _____

Describe what this season evokes in you. Example: *This season makes me feel invigorated, excited, like I can do anything.*

_____

_____.

What terrain *currently* attracts you the most? Examples: ocean with forest, ocean with desert, deep forest in the mountains, wild prairies.

_____

What does this terrain evoke in you? Example: *This terrain makes me feel wild and free, like I can really express myself.*

_____

_____.

If you could be a tree, what kind would you be? _____

Why? _____

_____

If you could be an animal, what kind would you be? _____

Why? _____

_____

If you could be a flower, what kind would you be? _____

Why? _____

_____

If you could be a specific aspect of nature (ocean, rain, lightning, mountain, meadow, cloud, lava, raindrop, pebble.) what would you be?

_____ Why? _____

_____

_____

In general, what feelings do all your selections evoke?

_____

What tangible things can you do in your life right now to elicit these feelings? Examples: spend more time in nature, grow a garden, hang nature pictures in your house, eat more fruits and vegetables. Perhaps the way to bring up these feelings is not necessarily directly attached to nature. Maybe it is about being creative or doing something in your life that makes you feel like you can breathe a little deeper. Maybe it is just sitting in the backyard alone under the stars.

_____

_____

_____

_____.

Healing and Balancing Exercise for Attuning with Nature. We all have healing ability—use it on yourself.

Place one hand beneath your navel.
Place the other hand on top of your head.
Concentrate deeply. Repeat silently or aloud for at least two minutes,
"I am nature; nature is me."

You have dissolved the feeling of being finite, feeling connected to the strength and beauty of nature.

Relaxation and Creative Visualization Exercise.

Lie in a comfortable position. Play instrumental music that makes you feel good: classical, new age, or music that is gentle, sweeping, or of dynamic beauty. When the music is playing, close your eyes. Inhale through your nose, and exhale through your mouth slowly, eight times. Visualize that you are inhaling the power of the universe, which purifies and attunes you: physically, emotionally, mentally, and metaphysically. When you exhale, all the tensions and worries leave your body and return to the universe where they dissolve and blend into the pure life force.

Tighten and loosen your muscles slowly in this order.

Feet. Tighten. Loosen. Take a slow, deep breath, and exhale.
Calves. Tighten. Loosen. Take a slow, deep breath, and exhale.
Thighs. Tighten. Loosen. Take a slow, deep breath, and exhale.
Hips and buttocks. Tighten. Loosen. Take a slow, deep breath, and exhale.
Stomach. Tighten. Loosen. Take a slow, deep breath, and exhale.
Back. Tighten. Loosen. Take a slow, deep breath, and exhale.
Arms. Tighten. Loosen. Take a slow, deep breath, and exhale.
Hands. Tighten. Loosen. Take a slow, deep breath, and exhale.
Neck and shoulders. Tighten. Loosen. Take a slow, deep breath, and exhale.
Face. Tighten. Loosen. Take a slow, deep breath, and exhale.

Then completely relax and take eight more slow, deep breaths. Inhale the universal life energy through your nose, and exhale tension through your mouth.

Set the intent: _Whoever I am, whatever I am, whatever I need, whatever is right for me—so be it. I open to insight. I open to receive._

Now that you are completely relaxed, give yourself over to the music that is playing. Allow the music to take you on a journey into aspects of nature. Be inside that aspect of nature, be it a leaf, a drop of water, a tree, an ocean, a cloud, a mountain, or a star. Experience it fully. What does it feel like? Be that aspect. Then, allow yourself to journey into other aspects of the natural world, and experience each fully, until the music comes to an end.

As the music ends, you know that you can draw upon the power of the natural world whenever you need, to revitalize, broaden life perspective, and receive strength. Rest a few minutes and bask in the experience.

Record your experience.

_____

_____

_____

_____

_____

_____

_____

_____

_____

_____

_____

_____

_____

_____

Draw a picture of yourself in the terrain that makes you feel good, or in the aspect of nature that helps heal and regenerate you. For example: You are in a cloud. Feel free to use colors, symbols, designs, or words.

Create a key phrase that summarizes the experience.

_____

When needed, say the mantra silently, and visualize the picture or symbol. This will generate a peaceful, empowered, and clear state of mind.

Δ
Gem of Wisdom

Self-worth is Intrinsic. No matter what you say or do, or what any other has said or done— worth is separate from all of that. We are all the same, yet magnificently individual: snowflakes unique, each one, yet together we create snow. Roses on a rose bush, separate, yes unique, but together we create the bush. We are pieces of a puzzle that together create the big picture of dark and light, yin and yang, tragedy and fortune. No one's perception, not even your own, can alter your worth or anyone else's.

Live the Mystery

17

WORKSHOP SEVENTEEN
THE BEAUTY OF IT ALL: YOUR PLACE IN THE WORLD

The bounty of life and its mysteries therein, can be known and lived by journeying into the rare and wondrous you. Self-examination also helps us better understand those around us, and the world in which we live. For at our core we are fundamentally the same. The more we understand our own behaviors and the motivations behind them, the more compassionate we will be toward others.

The human race is as one giant mobile. The movement of one person affects the whole pattern of movement of those around us, and in a sense, the world. Each being carries amazing importance, contributing to the full picture of the human experience. If we are affected adversely by the movement of those around us, we have the power to move ourselves in new ways that will positively change all our relationships, as well as making constructive contributions to the world.

There is no shame in anything we might discover about ourselves, and there is great reward in so doing. These discoveries enable us to stop worn out patterns from repeating and to write a healthy script for ourselves that will affect the rest of our lives. The beauty of it all is that we are not helpless, and that we can attain what we seek.

This is not selfishness. It is taking care of and being true to—ourselves. We each have a story to unfold, and adventure to be had. Every person and every story is equal in greatness and worth. Respect your story. Respect other people's stories.

The fruit of our efforts are felt most when we evolve ourselves rather than trying to change others. In this, we are loyal to our quintessential being, to our story, to this book of life we are trying to write, by living it. What is an adventure without dissonance? Would a book be read or a movie watched that had just ups and no downs, or good but no bad, right but no wrong, harmony but no chaos? If the characters in the movie or book sat around smiling all the time instead of meeting difficult challenges, the story would be dull. No one would grow. Labor spurs growth. Our life challenges make our life story *great*. When we triumph within, we sink into the blood beat of humanity. There is no greater story than that.

When you know who you are, and you are true to that—you help the whole world.

Write a mandate for yourself, titled "Who I am." Gather everything you have learned about yourself, both previously, and by doing this workbook. State boldly, clearly, and proudly who you are. Emblazon your discoveries into yourself. Hold them dear, always, and never forget that even in your weaknesses and faltering—you are more beautiful *because* of them. The smallest mottled leaf on a tree is no less important than the roots, trunk, or branches.

Appreciate your whole self, every particle, every trait: your face, your fingers, your molecules, your pain and your pleasure, your anger and compassion, sorrow and joy, fear and faith. Appreciate your ideas and your particular way of thinking. Appreciate your past, embrace the future, but always live in the present. You are who you are . . . and that is a great and wondrous thing.

Who I am.

_____

_____

_____

_____

_____

_____

_____

_____

_____

_____

_____

_____

_____

_____

_____

_____

_____

Healing and Balancing Exercise for Believing in Self. We all have healing ability—use it on yourself.

>**Place one hand over your heart.**
>**Place the other hand on the crown of your head.**
>**Concentrate deeply. Repeat silently or aloud for at least two minutes.**
>**"I am that I am."**

You can now embrace your core being, be true to it, and shine it into the world.

Relaxation and Creative Visualization Exercise.

Lie in a comfortable position. Play instrumental music that makes you feel good: classical, new age, or music that is gentle, sweeping, or of dynamic beauty. When the music is playing, close your eyes. Inhale through your nose, and exhale through your mouth slowly, eight times. Visualize that you are inhaling the power of the universe, which purifies and attunes you physically, emotionally, mentally, and metaphysically. When you exhale, all the tensions and worries leave your body and return to the universe where they dissolve and blend into the pure life force.

Tighten and loosen your muscles slowly in this order.

Feet. Tighten. Loosen. Take a slow, deep breath, and exhale.
Calves. Tighten. Loosen. Take a slow, deep breath, and exhale.
Thighs. Tighten. Loosen. Take a slow, deep breath, and exhale.
Hips and buttocks. Tighten. Loosen. Take a slow, deep breath, and exhale.
Stomach. Tighten. Loosen. Take a slow, deep breath, and exhale.
Back. Tighten. Loosen. Take a slow, deep breath, and exhale.
Arms. Tighten. Loosen. Take a slow, deep breath, and exhale.
Hands. Take a slow, deep breath, and exhale.
Neck and shoulders. Tighten. Loosen. Take a slow, deep breath, and exhale.
Face. Tighten. Loosen. Take a slow, deep breath, and exhale.

Then completely relax and take eight more slow, deep breaths. Inhale the universal life energy through your nose, and exhale tension through your mouth.

Set the intent: *Whoever I am, whatever I am, whatever I need, whatever is right for me—so be it. I open to insight. I open to receive.*

Now that you are completely relaxed, give yourself over to the music that is playing. Focus inward to your vast self, as vast as the universe. Journey within. Allow the music to take you on a free flight journey into yourself. The focus simply is that you are free to be you, and whoever you are, whatever you are . . . so be it. Whatever life is . . . so be it. You give yourself—to life. And you give yourself—to yourself. Whatever you need, in this experience now, you will receive. Then, without mental direction, see what happens. Watch, listen, feel. Go with the experience. If your body moves or vibrates, allow it. If words or a chant seem to form from your mouth—allow it. Trust yourself. Know that you have the power to heal your heart, and come into fruition. Just be.

As the music ends, take into your being, the whole universe, all of life. Know that while you are a unique individual, on another level you are also everything that exists. You will now feel this in your life, your individuality simultaneously with your connection to all. Rest a few moments, and bask in the experience.

Record your experience.

_____

_____

_____

_____

_____

_____

_____

_____

_____

_____

_____

_____

_____

_____

_____

_____

_____

Draw a picture or symbol that captures the experience.

Create a key phrase that summarizes the experience.

_____

When needed, say the mantra silently, and visualize the picture or symbol. This will generate a peaceful, empowered, and clear state of mind.

Δ

Gem of Wisdom

If you see yourself, you will see the world.
If you know yourself, you will know the world.
If you be yourself, you will become the world.

Live the Mystery

Congratulations!
You have completed Blue Wing Self-Discovery Workbook-Volume One.

About the Author

Susan D. Kalior was born in Washington State, raised in Phoenix, AZ. Her first profession was a psychotherapist (individual, marriage, and family counseling) treating those suffering from depression, anxiety, panic attacks, post-traumatic stress disorder, substance abuse, sexual abuse, family violence, and severe mental illness. She employed therapies such as communication skill building, relaxation training, systematic desensitization, bioenergetics, and psychodrama. She has worked in a mental hospital, a placement home for juvenile delinquents, and taught Kindergarten for a year. She has also facilitated numerous stress management, parenting, and self-discovery workshops (and still does) that have aided in the psycho-spiritual healing of many. Education and training include an M.A. in Ed. in Counseling/Human Relations and Behavior (NAU), a B.S. in Sociology (ASU), and ten months training at a Tibetan based community in Mesa Arizona (Staff Training Center) learning various psychotherapeutic methodologies and in-depth meditation techniques.

With her children grown, she is currently doing what she loves most: teaching self-discovery workshops, exploring the natural world, meditating, and writing educational and entertaining books that facilitate personal growth and transformation.

In her words: "I strive to see what is often missed, and to not miss what can't be seen. There is such a life out there, and in there—beyond all perception! So I close my eyes, feel my inner rhythm, and jump off the cliff of convention. And when I land, though I might be quaking in my boots, I gather my courage and go exploring.

Through travel, study, and work, I've gained a rich awareness of cultural differences among people and their psychosocial struggles. I have discovered that oppression often results from the unexamined adoption of outside perceptions. The healing always has been in the individual's stamina to expel outside perceptions of self and constructively exert one's unique core being into the world. I am driven to facilitate expanded awareness that people may separate who they are from who they are told to be. Embracing personal power by loving our unique selves in our weaknesses and strengths, in sickness and in health, for richer or poorer, for better or for worse . . . forever—is a key to joyous living. My motto is: Trust your story. Live the Mystery."